Library of
Davidson College

A
HISTORY OF MODERN HEBREW LITERATURE
(1785—1930)

BY

JOSEPH KLAUSNER Ph. D.

Professor of Modern Hebrew Language and Literature in the Hebrew University, Jerusalem

Authorised translation from the Hebrew by
HERBERT DANBY, D.D.

Edited by
LEON SIMON, C.B., B.A.

GREENWOOD PRESS, PUBLISHERS
WESTPORT, CONNECTICUT

The Library of Congress has catalogued this publication as follows:

Library of Congress Cataloging in Publication Data

Klausner, Joseph, 1874-1958.
   A history of modern Hebrew literature (1785-1930)

   "This translation [of Novo-evreĭskaia literatura] ... has been made from the Hebrew version published in 1920."
   1. Hebrew literature, Modern--History and criticism.
I. Title.
PJ5017.K513 1972   892.4'09   79-97289
ISBN 0-8371-2612-6

Originally published in 1932
by M. L. Cailingold, London

First Greenwood Reprinting 1972

Library of Congress Catalogue Card Number 79-97289

ISBN 0-8371-2612-6

Printed in the United States of America

CONTENTS

Editor's Preface I
Author's Introduction to the English
   Edition III
Chapter I
   The Beginnings of Modern Hebrew
   Literature 1
Chapter II
   The Romantic Period 21
Chapter III
   The Period of Realism 52
Chapter IV.
   The Period of Nationalism 83
Chapter V
   The Period of Revival 100
Chapter VI
   The More Recent Literature . . . 134
Glossary of untranslated terms . . . 195
Index 200

EDITOR'S PREFACE

The author of this Short History of Modern Hebrew Literature is himself a figure of note among Hebrew men of letters. Born in 1874, and educated first at the progressive *Yeshivah* of Odessa, Joseph Klausner was caught up at an early age in the new Hebrew movement, and it was under his influence and guidance that the friend of his boyhood, Saul Tchernichovsky (pp. 163-178), adopted Hebrew as the medium of his poetic genius. From 1897 to 1902 Klausner studied philosophy and Semitic languages at the University of Heidelberg. In 1903 he succeeded Ahad Ha-Am as editor of *Hashiloah* (pp. 125 6) which position he held until 1927, when the journal ceased to appear. In the meantime he had settled in Palestine, and in 1927 he became the first occupant of the Chair of Modern Hebrew Literature at the Jerusalem Hebrew University.

Klausner's main fields of interest lie in Jewish history, especially of the period of the Second Temple, and in modern Hebrew literature. His major Hebrew works include a *History of the Jewish People* from the earliest times to 73 C.E. (1909-1925); *The Messianic Idea in Jewish Life* (1909-1923); a *Life of Jesus* (1922), which has been translated into English and other languages; and the first volume of a large-scale *History of Modern Hebrew Literature* (1930). He has also written a large number of essays and occasional papers—some of which have been republished in form—on a wide variety of subject

II.

current problems of Zionism and Jewish nationalism, on which he holds pronounced views. There is, indeed, scarcely a single aspect of Jewish life, past or present, with which he has not dealt at one time or another. His devotion to research and his enormous erudition have never dried up the springs of an active and living interest in the present and its problems; and no mere dry-as-dust scholar could have influenced as he has done the younger generation of Hebrew writers, and the Jewish national movement in general. He has consistently upheld the ideal of a synthesis of Hebrew and humanistic culture. In his view the business of Hebrew literature is to express a distinctively Hebraic point of view; but this expression must cover the whole range of human interests. Hence he has always opposed the tendency to narrow the scope of Hebrew literature by restricting it to themes of specifically Jewish appeal. His standpoint is distinct from both the conservatism of Ahad Ha-Am and the radicalism of a Berditchewsky or a Brenner.

This translation of Dr. Klausner's book has been made from the Hebrew version published in 1920. The original text has been revised and to some extent amplified by the author for the purpose of the English version. In particular, he has added a brief section at the end to bring the book up to date.

A few of the verse quotations have been rendered into English verse by Miss Jessie E. Sampter, whose help is gratefully acknowledged. For the prose renderings of the remainder I am indebted to Mr. I. M. Lask.

LEON SIMON

LONDON: November, 1931

AUTHOR'S INTRODUCTION TO THE ENGLISH EDITION

The present work is a brief history of modern Hebrew literature, and is distinct from the writer's more detailed study of the same subject (*Historiah shel ha-Sifruth ha-Ivrith ha-Hadashah*, vol. I, Hebrew University Press, Jerusalem, 1930). Though the shorter study preceded the longer by many years, both were planned at the same time. The difference between them is not merely one of length and amplitude of detail. The longer work deals in detail with books and their authors, while the shorter is concerned solely with literary schools and currents of thought. The individual books and authors mentioned in the present work are introduced not so much for their own sake as to illustrate and bring into relief certain tendencies: for example, much is said of men like Zev Jawitz or Tchernichovsky, and little of men like Nahum Sokolow or Bernfeld. No attempt is made to appraise the intrinsic merits of the several works, but only to explain the sequence of the different schools and tendencies, which have succeeded one another as links in a single literary chain. This method of treatment throws into relief the various phases of modern Hebrew literature in the course of the last one hundred and fifty years, as well as the conflicts that have arisen in the religious and social life of the Jews throughout that period.

This is not without its importance. Not only Gentiles, but also Jews who are ignorant of Hebrew, still suppose that, although the Jews produced the Old Testament and the Talmud in a distant past, and perhaps something or other in the Middle Ages during their sojourn in Spain, yet their creative power came to an end when they left the Ghetto and began to enjoy equal rights with other nations. The present work may serve to show that even in this most recent period (1785-1930) the Jews have been struggling for existence and therefore creating new " cultural values "; and that this ancient people has not only a glorious past, but also a present that has its own value and holds out hope for the future

Translations of the present work have appeared in German (1921) and Italian (1926). (It was written first in Russian, 1900, second edition, 1912, and then issued afresh by the author in Hebrew, 1920.) These translations may, it is hoped, be of use as a source of information about the revived Hebrew language and literature; but they will be of far higher value in so far as they may pave the way to a better understanding of the Jewish people, and an appreciation of its share in the cultural progress of mankind. We Jews know the European races through their culture and literature; but they are completely ignorant of our modern literature. For them we are simply the people that once, in ancient days, produced the Hebrew Scriptures; they imagine that since then our creative powers have suffered extinction. The present volume may serve to correct this view. The "People of the Book" has not only created literature in the languages of the Gentiles among whom it lives, but still continues, in its national language, the creative work that covers thousands of years from Bible times to the present day. An understanding of this modern literature may help, perhaps, towards a better understanding of the race that produced it, and so bring the outside world nearer to the Jewish people—at least in so far as the outside world wrongs the Jews through ignorance, and can be led to right the wrong by fuller knowledge and a closer acquaintance.

JOSEPH KLAUSNER

JERUSALEM,
Marchesvan, 5692
(November, 1931)

CHAPTER I

THE BEGINNINGS OF MODERN HEBREW LITERATURE

The intellectual and rationalist movement of the 18th century originated in France, and thence spread to Germany. The Jews of Germany, like all Jews at that time, lived a self-centred life. Their dealings with Christians were confined to commerce; intellectual contact was entirely lacking. Their children were educated in *Heder* and *Yeshivah*; their books were written solely in Hebrew. They were under the sway of a religious ideal, which insisted on self-control and abstention from this world's pleasures. Romance was beyond their knowledge, and they were ignorant of the new life which was coming to birth in Europe. Any concern with foreign languages or general scientific studies was forbidden. Except for the debased German-Jewish jargon which they spoke, the only language permitted them was Hebrew, and even that was merely the " holy language." The single branch of learning that they might follow was the study of the Talmud and Talmudic commentaries. They might not even indulge overmuch in the study of the Prophets and the later books of the

Bible; and even the mediæval Hebrew philosophic literature was forbidden ground.

Consequently, when the intellectual movement began to spread among the Jews of Germany, there could be no question as to what language should be used as the vehicle for promulgating its ideas among the Jews: it was obvious that a new movement among Jews could and must be launched solely through the medium of Hebrew. Yet the advocates of the movement were innovators to the extent of conveying their message in a Hebrew style that belonged to the days of the Prophets: they broke away from the line of linguistic development that had produced post-Biblical Hebrew, the Hebrew of the Mishnah and of the literature of the Spanish period. The Hebrew writers of the end of the 18th century went far back to the primitive Hebrew of the Bible, although its predominantly poetical and rhapsodical character made it incapable of serving the needs of a modern literature. It was precisely this poetical strain in the language that attracted the early intellectuals, or *maskilim*. The dry style of rabbinic casuistry repelled them. They wanted a new style, with more beauty, freshness and vigour; and so they chose the language of the Prophets. They wiped out at a stroke the long post-Biblical period of development in order to revert to the language of Isaiah and Job.

In choosing the language of the Prophets

they had another object besides that of ridding themselves of the style of rabbinical casuistry. In the Prophets, those spirited champions of freedom and loathers of barren formalism and pointless religious routine, they found the stoutest opponents of ignorance and narrowness. The youthful exuberance of the Song of Songs, the quiet, simple dignity of the Book of Ruth, the charm of the narratives about kings, great popular leaders, lawgivers and seers—these were well fitted to breathe fresh life into the "dry bones," and to fill young Jews, cooped up in rabbinical seminaries and knowing nothing outside the Talmud and the ceremonial rules of Jewish life, with alluring dreams of mundane joys and of another life, fuller and more appealing. Though Hebrew was, as regards everyday speech, a "dead" language, it was in its youthful prime and vigour in the books of the Prophets and the divine poetry of Biblical story; hence, to read purely secular books in this ancient language, on subjects entirely novel, could not fail to create in the reader the impression of reading a truly living language, current among real people and serving as a means to that same end which in a measure was the ideal of the ancient Prophets.

But in this stylistic revival they went to extremes. To strengthen the impression that they were writing in a living language, they frequently lifted from the Bible whole sentences or phrases which had but the remotest relevance to the subject in hand. The result was that extraordinarily elusive style of writing known as *melitzah*, which, in its search after naturalness, achieved the acme of unnaturalness. Apart from this, it was obviously impossible to wipe out two thousand years of linguistic development and to go back to a language which was inadequate for everyday needs even in the era of the Second Temple.

We may regard the modern period of Hebrew literature as beginning in the year 1785, with the appearance of the first number of the periodical *Ha-Meassef*, in which the philosopher Moses MENDELSSOHN (1729-1786) collaborated. Some would date this epoch from Moses Hayyim LUZZATTO (1707-1747), the author of *The Tower of Strength* and *Praise be to the Righteous*; but he belongs rather to the preceding cabbalistic and mystical era.

Ha-Meassef served a double purpose: to spread "enlightenment" (*Haskalah*, *Aufklärung*) among the Jews, and to cultivate the Hebrew language, or, rather, to foster literary taste and feeling for good style. One of its most diligent editors and contributors was Moses Mendelssohn's biographer, Isaac EUCHEL (1756-1804). This versatile author ridiculed current Jewish prejudices and declaimed against the follies and superstitions that had accumulated around the Jewish religion. The idea which he especially emphasized was that *Haskalah* was not incompatible with genuine, instructed religious belief. The same idea appears in the scholarly articles of Baruch LINDAU (1759-1849), the author of *First Principles of Learning*, a work on natural history. Other regular contributors to *Ha-Meassef* included Judah Löb BEN ZEV (1764-1811), author of a well-known Hebrew grammar, *Talmud Leshon Ivri*, and Isaac SATANOV (1732-1804); but the most remarkable and accomplished of the writers of that generation was Naphtali Hirsch WEIZL, or Wessely (1725-1805), a friend of Moses Mendelssohn. He first made his name as a philologian (*Gan Na'ul*, 1765), and as one of the producers of the *Bi'ur* ("Explanation"), which was an edition of the Hebrew Bible with a modern German translation in keeping with the spirit of the time, and with explanatory notes and an introduction in Hebrew. This translation, done in collaboration with Moses Mendelssohn by a group of younger scholars (Solomon Dubno, Ben Zev, Brüll and others), revolutionised the attitude of the younger Jewish generation towards the Bible and the language in which it was composed. Through this translation and commentary, they learned to appreciate the lofty moral standards of the Bible, and the beauty and dignity of the ancient Hebrew language. Moreover, the German translation made a knowledge of German possible to those Yiddish-speaking Jews who knew no other language but Hebrew. Thus through the medium of the "dead" Hebrew many of them came to know the living German.

The more fanatical Jews raised a great outcry against this translation, realising that it was likely to lead the younger generation out of the " straight path," since it would estrange them from Talmudic casuistry and teach them to understand the Bible in a manner not at all in keeping with the traditional and accepted interpretations. At about the same time, Joseph II's " Edict of Toleration " appeared (January 2, 1782), summoning the Jews of Austria to accept modern ideas and promising them equal rights. This edict also the orthodox regarded with deep suspicion. It was at this stage that WESSELY entered the field. He was both deeply religious and an advocate of modern learning. He wrote (1762) *Divré Shalom v'Emeth*, " Words of Peace and Truth" (1782), which, with its novel views on Hebrew education, was attacked by the orthodox, while the *Maskilim* rallied in its defence. Wessely became the idol and the trusted leader of the younger generation. His fame and popularity were greatly enhanced by his poem *Shiré Tif'ereth*, " Songs of Glory," which, in rhapsodical style and rhymed verse, after the fashion of the contemporary European poets, described Israel's great lawgiver, Moses, the chief of the Prophets, the exodus of the Jews from Egypt and their wanderings in the wilderness. In the main it was nothing more than a recital in verse of stories out of the Pentateuch, in the pseudo-classical manner affected in Europe at the time; and the influence of Klopstock's great poem, *Messiade*, is obvious. It affords nothing new in its outlook on the Biblical events, or in imaginative scope or vigour of language, and it is now as wearisome and uninteresting as the *Messiade* itself. But just as Klopstock, now almost completely forgotten, counted as the father of German poetry, so Wessely is to be reckoned the father of modern Hebrew poetry. His tinkling rhymes and his rich and rhapsodical Biblical language were at that time something new and unheard of; for till then Hebrew literature had been wholly taken up with moral and exegetical treatises and rabbinic *responsa*, insipid in content and vapid in manner and style.

In contrast to the other writers in *Ha-Meassef*, Wessely was almost the only one to occupy himself with specifically Jewish subjects. Most of the others busied themselves with translations of unimportant works from the German : anything was good enough so long as it was far removed from abstract theory and Talmudic Judaism. Hence they produced not a single Hebrew work of national value, and left behind them nothing of interest to posterity.

Among the contributors to *Ha-Meassef* was a playwright, David FRANCO (Hofshi)-MENDES (1713-1792), of Amsterdam, a Sephardi Jew of Marrano descent, who also dealt with topics of Hebrew interest. He wrote a play, *Athaliah's Requital*, in imitation of Racine and Metastasio, and a series of biographies of distinguished Spanish-Portuguese Jews of the Middle Ages. Here also he was an exception, since most of the contributors to *Ha-Meassef* did nothing beyond translating the fables, idylls, and love-poems of German writers. So it was that among the Jews of Germany Hebrew literature stopped short at its very beginning: the next generation of Jewish authors began to write in German, and they have gone on doing so ever since.

The development of modern Hebrew literature in Austria, more particularly in Galicia, began somewhat later and took a different course. It did not rest content with poetry and *belles-lettres*. Something more intellectual was needed to divert the younger generation from dry Talmudical casuistry, and to provide an adequate substitute for religious faith, which was weakening, and for the study of the Law, which was losing its appeal. This ideal was foremost in the mind of the learned Solomon Judah RAPOPORT (1790-1867).

Rapoport was the father of the so-called

"Science of Judaism," i.e., the scientific study of Jewish history, Hebrew philology, and the philosophy of Judaism. The Talmud and Talmudic commentaries had long been deemed above criticism, and had been studied as a religious exercise. Henceforth this attitude of simple acceptance was to give place to critical and historical research into the whole of the ancient literature, Talmudical works included. Rapoport collected together a wealth of material, which he subjected to scholarly criticism and analysis, and was thus able to estimate afresh the merits of outstanding Jewish authors and writings, religious customs, national institutions, and the like. By a comprehensive range of studies in the lives of mediæval Jewish scholars and poets (among them R. Eliezer ha-Kalir, R. Saadiah, R. Nathan of Rome), which testify to their author's learning and acumen, he laid the foundation for the later researches of Zunz, Jost, Geiger, and Graetz.

Resident in Galicia and almost contemporary with Rapoport was the still more profound and original scholar, Nachman KROCHMAL (1785-1840). He wrote but one work, *The Modern Guide to the Perplexed**, published posthumously (1851) by Zunz. This profound work outlines a philosophy of Jewish history. The author was an able

---

*Maimonides had called his great work, written with a similar purpose nearly seven centuries earlier, *The Guide to the Perplexed*.

disciple of contemporary German philosophers, and interpreted Jewish history in the spirit of Hegel's interpretation of universal history. In the evolution of humanity Hegel perceived the embodiment of "universal mind," working through the three logical processes of "thesis," "antithesis," and "synthesis." Krochmal perceived the embodiment of the fundamentally unchangeable " spiritual-absolute " of Israel at work in the recurrent drama of the life of the Jewish race : the race grows up, develops, and then withers, so that it becomes virtually dead and ceases to exist; it revives again, grows up, develops once again until it once more withers, and so on, again and again. But its "spiritual-absolute" neither perishes nor ceases to function. Such is the secret of the nation's survival and of its permanence.

After Judah Ha-Levi in his work *Ha-Kuzari*, Nachman Krochmal and his son, Abraham Krochmal, were the first to put forward the idea of the " mission of Israel," which is to impose the rule of a " higher righteousness " on humanity, and to reform the world by the " reign of the Almighty," the reign of " absolute morality." Like Judah Ha-Levi, they inculcated a faith in the eternity of Israel and in its national destiny. Nachman Krochmal's work contains, moreover, a wealth of original views on Jewish history, and also the elements of Biblical criticism, in which he had been anticipated in Hebrew literature only by Ibn Ezra (to whom Krochmal devoted an important section of his great work, entitled *Hokmat ha-Misken*—" The Wisdom of the Poor "). Galician Hebrew literature was not monopolised by scholars : to it belongs also the first Hebrew satirist, Isaac ERTER (1792-1851). He wrote but a handful of articles and sketches, collected after his death and published under the title *Watchman of the House of Israel* (1858); but what pungency, acuteness, and vital truth are hidden away in these few pages! Whatever left his pen was pregnant with a spirit of stinging and deep-cutting humour and satire, now thundering its vigorous protest, now laughing through its tears. Erter mercilessly criticised ignorant superstition, and bitterly mocked the pseudo-piety of the Hasidim and their miracle-mongers. He rose in passionate revolt against the hypocrites and pretended pietists, who held that if only a Jew observed the religious ceremonial laws, he was free to ignore moral obligations. He protested against cabbalistic mysticism and the superstitious follies which had choked the pure well of Jewish faith; he held up to ridicule the tortuous dealings of the *Tzaddiks* and *Rebbis* and the cabbalistic beliefs in good and evil spirits, which are utterly foreign to genuine Judaism. Nor did he spare the older established rabbinical authorities and the religious students with their petrified methods and minds; nor yet the Jewish community officials, who lent the weight of their authority to the false guides, and cared for nothing but their own profit and position. All this ridicule and satire was clothed in a brilliant Biblical Hebrew style, surpassing in its trenchancy, elegance and polish anything previously written in modern Hebrew.

It is difficult to convey any idea of the impression made by Erter's *Watchman* on the type of Jewish youth that frequented the rabbinical seminaries—the only educated Jewish public then to be found in eastern Europe. For the first time their eyes were opened to the festering wounds in the Hebrew body politic; for the first time they realised that outside the Ghetto there was coming about a "transvaluation of values," that a new life was in the making, freed from the trammels of tradition and full of new sensibilities, new longings, new conceptions, new ideas, and new demands. Orthodox circles were aware that this book aimed at breaking down the old traditional manner of life; and so they forbade their children to read any "uncanonical literature" and, more particularly, this book of Erter's. They condemned the book to be burnt as a heretical work, and they severely punished anyone suspected of reading it. But stolen waters are sweet; and nothing, perhaps, served more to give an impetus to the circulation of Erter's book than the ban placed upon it by the orthodox, and the persecutions endured by its readers.

Yet another Galician Hebrew satirist was Joseph PERL (1773-1839), founder of the first modern Hebrew school, in Tarnopol. In his *Megalleh Temirin*, " Revealer of Secrets," published in 1819 under the pseudonym Jacob Obadiah ben Petachiah, he attacked Hasidism with the weapons used by the authors of the *Epistolæ obscurorum virorum* in their attack on Roman Catholic hypocrisy : in the form of letters from one Hasid to another, there is laid bare before us all the barbarous ignorance of the Hasidim, all the crudity of their lives, their language, and their outlook. The expression " Megalleh Temirin language " is still a figure of speech for language that is corrupt and crude.

Erter was survived by a like-minded fellow-worker in Joshua Heschel SCHORR (1814-1895). With Erter's collaboration, Schorr established the literary annual *He-Halutz*, which he continued to edit for many years after Erter's death. Schorr was exceptionally gifted, of an independent cast of mind, vigorous in expressing his unorthodox notions, and always an extremist in his views. He spent his life in the study of ancient Hebrew literature, not in the interests of pure scholarship, but always with an eye to present social needs and problems. Together with Abraham KROCHMAL (1823-1888), the son of Nachman Krochmal, he brought a vigorous and impartial criticism to bear on the beliefs and ideas of the Talmud. He even permitted himself liberties with the text of the Bible, in which he made emendations that ran counter to accepted tradition. Thus a breach was made in the solid wall of Judaism, and perhaps too great a breach for that time of day. It did not occur to these iconoclasts and fighters that one day the stormy course of history might once again drive the Jews back into the Ghetto, and that then the Ghetto walls, thus weakened, might not be able to withstand the strange and evil blasts let loose in the world, still less to afford protection to those within.

Apart from a large number of versifiers, there was one gifted poet among the makers of Hebrew literature in Galicia at that time, Meir Halevi LETTERIS (1800-1871). He is known mainly by his translation of the plays of Racine on subjects drawn from the Bible, his famous imitation of *Faust*, published under the title *Ben Abuyah*, and his translation of Byron's *Hebrew Melodies*. Thus, unlike most of the Hebrew poets in Germany, he chose for translation works of Jewish interest. He also wrote many original poems on Jewish subjects. Most notable is his national poem, *The Mourning Dove*, for which a sad and tender musical setting was composed. Letteris, like the ancient Jewish sages, likens the congregation of Israel to a

simple dove, expelled from her nest, wandering to and fro in strange places, and finding no resting place. The dove prays to her Saviour and Redeemer to restore her to her own nest, her own country:
Return, life of my spirit! Return, my comfort! Give heed to my bitter lament, conduct me to my habitation. Pity me, the forsaken one, give me back thy love; return to the clefts of my rock, and I will shelter beneath thy wings.

All these Galician scholars and writers contributed to the current literary annuals— *Bikkuré ha-Ittim,* 12 vols., 1821-1832, founded by Shalom Hakohen; *Kerem Hemed,* 9 vols., 1833-1856, edited by S. L. Goldenberg and the famous scholar Senior Sachs (1816-1892); *He-Halutz,* by Schorr, and *Otzar Nehmad,* by Blumenfeld, all of which were continuations of *Ha-Meassef,* though they preserved a more scholarly atmosphere and the *Melitzah* style was less pronounced. The second and third of these annuals contained important contributions from the well-known Reform Rabbi and scholar, Abraham GEIGER (1810-1874), written in a lucid and fluent Hebrew style.

The literary annual *Bikkuré ha-Ittim* published contributions from a noted Italian Jew, whose abilities entitle him to rank higher than almost any of those hitherto mentioned, with the exception of Nachman Krochmal. This was Samuel David LUZZATTO (1800-1865). There is hardly a branch of

Jewish thought or activity on which he did not exert a marked influence : Hebrew philology, poetry, religious philosophy, archæology, history, the discussion of current problems—in all these fields he made valuable contributions, and in some of them his achievement was nothing short of astonishing.

In certain respects S. D. Luzzato was a child of his time, but in others he was ahead of all contemporary writers and scholars. He lived during the period of reaction against 18th-century pseudo-classicism and rationalism, and assimilated the point of view of the best contemporary thinkers. Thus he was entirely opposed to the rationalist interpretation of the Bible, and sharply criticised the emendations of Schorr and the negative attitude assumed by Jost (the first historian of Judaism and the forerunner of Graetz) towards the historical foundations of Biblical and Talmudic Judaism. He had the courage to criticise even Maimonides himself, the greatest Jewish philosopher of the Middle Ages. For the first time in the Hebrew literature of the *Haskalah*, he gave expression to the view that faith and knowledge, which Maimonides tried to reconcile by compromise, are mutually antagonistic : unity between them is impossible, since the very basis and breath of religion is emotional fervour, whereas knowledge demands detached apprehension and reasoned analysis. Faith has no use for intellectual apprehension, just as knowledge has no use for acceptance on trust. That alone can rank as knowledge which can be tested in the crucible of experience, or is capable of logical proof; but that which has been examined and proved makes no call on faith. Luzzatto also opposed Maimonides because of his attempt to find a harmony between Judaism and Hellenism, between Moses and Aristotle. According to Luzzatto, Judaism and Hellenism are two opposites: they are permanently at war and incapable of consorting together. Judaism has its foundation in the feeling for righteousness and justice, in fervour and devotion; whereas Hellenism has its foundation in the feeling for beauty, in sensuality and rationalism. According to Luzzatto, knowledge cannot bring man happiness: " absolute morality " alone can bestow complete inward happiness on human society. The origin of such exalted morality is not in the works of Aristotle, but in the books of the Prophets; and it was from the Prophets that Christianity also drew its ethical system, although, according to Luzzatto, by adding to its teaching ascetic principles, and admitting many Hellenistic elements, it has achieved the contrary of what it set out to achieve.

Luzzatto's standpoint vindicates not only the claim of the Jews to a nationality of their own, but also the claims of their religion and its ceremonial laws. In his view, the poetry of Jewish custom and the lofty ethical system of ancient Judaism are threatened with extinction by the revival of Hellenism in modern Europe; and the duty and the possibility of defending and maintaining them belong to the Jewish people alone.

What Luzzatto found admirable in religion was not its stereotyped creeds, but its poetry and its exalted morality. Hence he was not in favour of abolishing religious customs and ceremonial laws: for him they were as the wick of the " perpetual lamp " which illuminates the world, the lamp of righteousness and justice, of equality and humanity. The wick itself may be a thing of no account, but without it light and heat are impossible. Luzzatto united scholarship with a faith as deep as that of the contemporary French " romantics," though he had none of their emotionalism or rhetorical pathos.

He wrote an Italian translation of the Scriptures with a Hebrew commentary, and in the course of years of searching in museums and libraries discovered early manuscripts of the Spanish-Jewish poets, which he published with valuable introductions and notes. His favourite poet, and the one most akin to him in spirit, was Judah Ha-Levi, who cultivated philosophy as well as poetry, and in his *Ha-Kuzari* maintained that the basis and root of Judaism was emotion and morality, not dry dogmatism and frigid rationalism. In particular, he edited Judah Ha-Levi's nationalist-Zionist poems. In his letters Luzzatto speaks sympathetically and hopefully of the gradual settlement of Jewish agriculturists in Palestine, and his *Kinnor Na'im* includes nationalist poems which might well have been written by a fervent Zionist of to-day. In this respect he was far in advance of most of his contemporaries.

His prose style, too, was almost unique in his generation. Discarding the stilted Biblical idiom then in vogue, he preferred the clearness and simplicity of post-Biblical Hebrew, and developed a style akin to that of Rashi, the great medieval commentator, whom he much admired for his unsophisticated faith and his light, easy style.

Among the better-known Italian Hebrew writers are Isaac Samuel REGGIO of Goritzia (1789-1860), author of many works on Cabbalah and theology (*The Law from Heaven, The Law and Philosophy*, etc.), in which he sought a compromise between the Jewish Law and philosophy, though he opposed Cabbalah; and a kinswoman of Luzzatto, the poetess Rachel MORPURGO (1790-1870), some of whose poems were translated into German by the Austrian Jewish poet Ludwig August Frankl.

S. D. Luzzatto had many disciples in Italy (among whom may be mentioned Issac Hayyim CASTIGLIONE and Ehud LOLLI) but he had a still greater influence on Hebrew writers in

Eastern Europe. His originality and the soundness of his methods were not fully recognized until a generation later, when the ideas of Jewish nationalism had become widespread. During his lifetime he was no more than a poet and scholar of repute; after his death he came into his own as a force in Jewish life and a Hebrew writer of national importance.

CHAPTER II
THE ROMANTIC PERIOD

In Russia modern Hebrew literature began later than in Austria and Italy, and the earliest examples of modern Hebrew did not appear until the third decade of the 19th century. The influence of the German-Jewish intellectual movement and of the *Bi'ur* are very obvious in the works of the first three Hebrew writers, whose period of literary activity coincides with the reign of Nicholas I. These three, the " threefold cord," were the scholar and propagandist Isaac Dov (Bär) LEVINSOHN, the journalist and satirist Mordecai Aharon GUNZBURG, and the poet Abraham Dov Hakohen LEBENSOHN (known as Adam Hakohen—*A*braham *D*ov *M*ikhailishki, after the name of the town where he lived for a time after marriage. He was born and passed most of his life in Vilna).

Isaac Dov LEVINSOHN (1788-1860), born in Kremenitz, a small town in Volhynia, played an important rôle not only in modern Hebrew literature, but also in the dissemination of *Haskalah* among the Jews of Russia. At the beginning of the 19th century, when Levinsohn began his literary work, the Jews of Russia and Poland were so far removed from even the most elementary idea of general culture that they regarded all "external" knowledge, including the knowledge of a non-Jewish language, as something fraught with grave danger to Judaism. They feared that secular knowledge would estrange their sons from the study of the Talmud and from "the straight path." Nor was their opposition confined to foreign languages: they even banned the study of Hebrew as an ordinary language with definite grammatical rules and a modern secular literature. The ancient Hebrew language, and the religious literature written in it, they regarded as holy; and in the use of modern Hebrew for modern needs they saw a source of corruption, a poisonous root of heresy, atheism and anti-Judaism. In the opinion of the orthodox it was forbidden even to learn Hebrew grammar or to study the Prophets and later books of the Bible; and now that the modern Hebrew authors in Germany and Austria had discovered in lyric poetry, in criticism and in satire, an antidote to the disease of exclusive application to Talmudical casuistry and religious studies, the orthodox came to regard even the Bible itself (except the Pentateuch), and anything written in Biblical Hebrew, as forbidden things.

Prejudices of this kind were not the only evil fruit of the Ghetto life. Because in the Middle Ages Jews were not allowed to engage in husbandry, and in the Ghetto their choice of occupations was limited to trade and the study of the Talmud, the odd idea became widespread among them that it was unseemly for the " chosen people " to work on the land, and that handiwork of any sort was degrading to a Jew. Levinsohn, well versed both in ancient Hebrew literature and in general knowledge, launched a campaign against these prejudices; and since the Jews of the time relied entirely on religious books, from which they derived the wildest and most fantastic notions, he decided to fight them with their own weapons. He sought and found in the Talmud and the Midrashim, and in mediæval Hebrew religious literature, numerous sayings and expressions which made it perfectly obvious that a knowledge of foreign languages and general subjects of learning (and still more, a knowledge of Hebrew and its grammar and literature), so far from being regarded as a sin, was actually a sacred obligation laid on every Jew who wished to understand the nature of his religion and faith and to be convinced of the genuineness of its foundation. He showed that the very sages of the Talmud themselves knew foreign languages and various sciences, and learned much from Greek and Roman writers, and that husbandry and manual labour were frequently commended in the Talmud and later literature; while as for handicrafts, many of the Sages of the Talmud were themselves craftsmen and artisans— Rabbi Jochanan was a cobbler, Rabbi Isaac a blacksmith, and so forth.

Levinsohn's books, *Te'udah b'Israel* and *Beth Yehudah*, were written in a very easy, popular style. He was not an original or profound scholar, and his learning was neither wide nor systematic: he was entirely self-taught and had no schooling. But he knew how to set forth such learning as he had in a manner appropriate to the needs of the vital purpose he had set before himself, and also intelligibly to the contemporary Hebrew reader. To such a reader Levinsohn's books unfolded a lively picture of the historical development of the laws and customs of Israel, with a description of the economic and political condition of the Jews at various epochs. Thus the reader learned to understand which Jewish customs could be accounted fundamental, from the point of view of Jewish religion and culture, and which secondary and superfluous, a mere painful inheritance imposed on Judaism during the Middle Ages, as a result of persecutions from without and of the confined life within the Ghetto.

Levinsohn's was defensive and not aggresive warfare: he did not attack religion, but stood in defence of the new ideals of the generation of *Haskalah*. Hence his books succeeded in winning many of those who, while retaining their religious connections, were not excessively orthodox or fanatical. His books never attack what is important and fundamental in Judaism. He employed the weapons of Erter—poems and satirical sketches—against the vagaries of the Cabbalah and the wonder-working *Tzaddicks* of the Hasidim; but whatever he regarded as essentially and fundamentally Jewish was for him sacred, and he would never lay the finger of criticism upon it.

While Levinsohn thus tried to convince the orthodox Jews of the need for European culture and closer relations with the Christians, he also defended his people against the attacks of all manner of Jew-haters and opponents of Judaism. It must be remembered that Levinsohn lived and worked during the reign of Nicholas I, at a time when the Russian government scarcely knew the Jews at all, and the attacks of the anti-Semites were directed not so much against the Jewish people as against the Jewish religion and its ancient literature. Levinsohn replied to these attacks on the Talmud in a number of well-informed and temperately written books, such as *Zerubbabel* and *Ahijah the Shilonite*. In his *Efes Damim* he dealt with the scandalous and ridiculous "blood accusation." This timely and useful book was twice translated into Russian, and also into German and English. At the same time, as we have seen, Levinsohn carried on the fight against Jewish obscurantism, and especially against the Hasidic *Rebbis*, in pungent satirical verse. In *Beth ha-Otzar* and

Oholé Shem he entered the field of Hebrew philology; but these, like the rest of his purely scholarly works, are somewhat unsystematic and prolix, and give a general impression of amateurishness. The second modern Hebrew author, who exerted an influence scarcely less than that of Levinsohn on the spread of the *Haskalah* movement among the Jews and on the development of Hebrew literature, was Mordecai Aaron GUNZBURG (1795-1846), the leader of the "Vilna intellectuals." His method was different from Levinsohn's. He did not take up the cudgels on behalf of *Haskalah*, but introduced the very spirit of *Haskalah* into Hebrew literature. He was a many-sided author, and wrote in Hebrew on anything and everything: on the geography of Palestine, on the Samaritans, on the French in Russia (1813), on the need for reform in Hebrew education (*Abiezer*). He translated into Hebrew a book by the German author Zschokke which had nothing to do with Judaism at all; he also translated a work so important for Judaism as Philo's "Embassy to the Emperor Caius Caligula." He wrote in Hebrew an able *History of the Russians*, and published the first volume of a universal history entitled *The Story of Man*, which had a wide circulation because of the novelty of such a book in Hebrew. His guiding principle was that a little light dispels much darkness. A direct attack on obscurantism is unprofitable: let light into the dark alleys, and the darkness will disappear of itself. He realised that the younger generation needed only a correct idea of the history of the country and people in and among which they lived to develop the desire and the will to learn the language of this people and country; and that the Talmudic Jews needed only some idea of general history to be convinced that the Talmud and its commentaries were not the alpha and omega of all learning and human knowledge. And, in fact, despite persecution from the orthodox, Günzburg's works, like those of Erter and Levinsohn, found their way surreptitiously into all the *Heders, Yeshivahs* and other resorts of Jewish youth. The spirit of freshness and youth in these new little books, their charm, their simplicity and their novelty at once throw into relief the shortcomings of the older literature, with all the difficulty and mustiness of its ponderous tomes.

In his autobiographical sketch, *Abiezer*, Günzburg has given us a clear picture of the old-fashioned manners and customs of his generation, which had such a pernicious effect on the education of children both at school and in the home. It was realised that the time had come for radical changes in Judaism, and that the modern Hebrew authors who were fighting the battle of *Haskalah* must soon change their defensive tactics for more aggressive methods. But first of all it was necessary to prepare the ground, to educate the Hebrew reader's taste and to make him more susceptible to all that enlarges the beauty and fulness of life. Briefly, what was needed was the rejuvenating influence of a new "melodious burst" of poetry, which had been so near to the Jewish heart in olden times, and even in the Spanish epoch, but had fallen into eclipse during the last three hundred years. And new poets appeared. They gave a new outlook on life to the younger generation of Jews, and laid solid foundations for the new Hebrew literature, which thenceforward was to find its place—perhaps without any such intention on the part of its creators—not merely as a means for the spread of *Haskalah*, but as a national possession and a necessary condition of national life for the Jewish people.

The first of this new school of poets was Abraham Dov Hakohen LEBENSOHN (Adam Hakohen), a native of Vilna, where he spent the better part of his life, at first in association with Günzburg, and afterwards as the centre of a large group of authors and poets, over whom he exerted a powerful influence. He was born in Vilna in 1794, and died at a ripe old age in 1878. He was a born poet, who both felt keenly and thought deeply; but he lacked a broad intellectual background, and he spent his entire life in the narrow atmosphere of the elementary teacher and the petty trader. Past his youth before he became acquainted with secular literature, he never properly learned a single European language. It may be matter for debate whether a poet's native endowment, however great, can carry him through without education and breadth of culture; but there can be no doubt that a poet whose best years have been spent in the study of dry religious literature is in urgent need of some æsthetic education if he is to shake off the habit of casuistry and philosophising. Such education Adam Hakohen never acquired. Hence we find in his poems an excessive tendency to philosophise, which every now and again deadens his lively and powerful poetical sense.

That he did possess an original and strong poetical sense is evident from his profoundly moving poem *Compassion*. Here we have the anguished and heart-rending cry of a soul that is racked by the *Weltschmerz*, the endless suffering which in its diverse forms dogs mankind everywhere and always. In everything the poet sees destruction and desolation; he feels the nothingness and the aimlessness of existence, the brevity of imaginary human happiness, the limitations and the feebleness of human understanding; and his feeling finds expression in rich and vigorous lines written in a correct and lucid Biblical style. The figurative and concrete language of the Prophets becomes under his pen an extraordinarily appropriate instrument for the expression of lofty philosophical and poetical ideas of extreme abstractness and subtlety. Even now, when most of the subjects of Adam Hakohen's poems have become more or less antiquated, it is impossible to read without deep emotion such a poem as his *Pessimist and Optimist*. The pessimist begins his indictment thus:

> Did I but know that my voice could destroy the world and the fullness thereof with all the hosts of Heaven, I would raise a mighty cry, " Let there be rest!" and return to the void together with all that lives.

And, as might be expected of a true poet, the description of the darker side of life far surpasses the optimist's picture of the happiness and pleasures of this world and the preordained purpose of human existence.

Adam Hakohen's *Dal Mevin* (" The Poor Sage ") was very widely read. It shows the advantage of poverty over wealth: peace of mind, health-giving labour, and the like. This song was sung for years in many a Lithuanian town, and every devotee of Hebrew literature knew it by heart.

Adam Hakohen mostly found his themes in the realm of abstract philosophico-poetical questions, and his poetry very rarely touched on the problems of contemporary Jewish life. In the 'forties and 'fifties of last century this was a very dangerous subject: the orthodox were then in the ascendant, and Adam Hakohen, who was first a school-teacher and afterwards a small trader, was dependent on them. It was not until he had reached old age, in 1866, and was a teacher in the Vilna rabbinical college, that he published an allegorical play, *Truth and Faith*, modelled as to its form on Moses Hayyim Luzzatto's *Tower of Strength* and *Praise be to the Righteous*, in which he pours ridicule both on the superstitions of religious orthodoxy, and on the corruption of manners and morals that was hidden behind the mask of religion. Its hero, Tziveon, closely resembles Molière's Tartuffe, except that the Hebrew Tartuffe, in addition to the qualities which Molière bestowed on his hero, has a special Jewish characteristic: a barren casuistry based on distortion of scriptural texts. Adam Hakohen also deals faithfully with the " holy simplicity " characteristic of the Jewish masses, who will blindly follow after any hypocritical charlatan. But he never gibes at religious faith, for in his opinion honest intellectualism, true *Haskalah*, is no foe of genuine religion.

This book appeared at a time when attacks on hypocrisy and ignorant superstition were already common form in Hebrew literature; but his *Songs in the Holy Language*, published as far back as 1842, caused a great sensation in the ranks of the orthodox, although at first sight they appear quite innocuous. Till then no Hebrew author in Russia had dared to strike out a new line, and the orthodox at once suspected that these poems, which had much to say in praise of wisdom and the value of reason, and dared to put knowledge on a level with religion, were a serious menace to religious dogma. The danger was the greater in that their appeal was not to the intelligence only, but also to the emotions of the younger generation; and, indeed, the emotional awakening of the young Talmudic students was the main work of the elder Lebensohn.

A much greater influence was, however, exerted in this direction by his son and pupil, Micah Joseph LEBENSOHN (1828-1852). This poet, who showed signs of great genius, died at the early age of twenty-four, after a life full of trouble and suffering. Towards the end of his life, when his poetical activity had but begun, he developed consumption, which brought his life to a premature end. He was given one advantage denied to his father in that he received a fair intellectual and æsthetic training. He knew German better than his father ever did, and he had a great admiration and reverence for his favourite poet, Schiller. In Berlin he attended the lectures of Schelling in natural philosophy, and there he made the acquaintance of two prominent Hebraists, Leopold Zunz and Senior Sachs, at whose suggestion it was that he drew on Jewish history in his choice of subjects for poetical treatment.

He left behind him three books: *The*

Destruction of Troy, a fine Hebrew translation (from Schiller's version) of that part of the *Aeneid* which contains the episode of the Wooden Horse; *Shiré bath Tziyon,* "Songs of the Daughter of Zion," containing six poems on subjects drawn from ancient and mediæval Jewish history; and, finally, *Kinnor bath Tziyon,* "The Lyre of the Daughter of Zion," a collection of his short poems published posthumously by his aged father, who survived him. These small volumes, and particularly the second and third, rank with the best of modern Hebrew poetry. The first of the six historical *Songs* is entitled *Solomon and Ecclesiastes*. According to tradition, Solomon wrote both the Song of Songs and the book Ecclesiastes, and the contrast between them—between the hymn to love and beauty, which reaches the height of youthful passion and abandon in the rapturous "How fair and how pleasant art thou, O love, for delights," and the testament of pessimism, which touches the depths of despair and doubt in its bitter cry, "Vanity of vanities, all is vanity!" and its constantly repeated "Who knoweth?"—this striking contrast fascinated the young poet and stirred him to write his poem. The first section shows us the youthful Solomon, happy and filled with longings and desires. He falls in love with the shepherdess, Shulamith, and in the young lover's ardent heart her beauty blends with the beauty of nature, unrolling in majestic splendour on the hillsides of Judah and Ephraim. With their first kiss there bursts forth the young prince's first song, the entrancing vision, brimful of love, the immortal Song of Songs. He refuses to believe in man's wickedness, in pain or tears of sorrow:

> In the strength of his passion he thinks that there is no such thing as grief, that man's life is all love and rejoicing. How can all sorrow not be brought to an end, and Death be swallowed up, when he and his love are so happily mated?

In these words, depicting the young man's joyful outlook, there yet lurks the seed of his future despair. Solomon the happy is also Solomon the wise. In his youth wisdom enhances happiness, but in his old age it brings him only pain and anguish of heart. His wisdom conquers his faith and puts it to flight, leaving but the one bitter question, "Who knoweth?" Wisdom impels Solomon irresistibly to analyse, to search, to probe, and so kills all spontaneous feeling. He loses his faith in love; beauty has no more charm for him. These beautiful eyes, what are they but veins and sinews? These rosy cheeks, what are they but tissues streaked with blood? The rose and the lily and the bluebell are nothing but "decaying beauty, blooms of death." The soul—that too may be nothing but a more or less complex mechanism, compounded of dead matter, of "blood and marrow." Innocence and guilt depend merely on a change that comes about in a single vein through the withdrawal of a single drop of blood:

> Take but one drop of blood from the proud sinner, and he might become righteous and humble; and haply the honest man might do foul villainies, were but one sinew of his heart to be changed.

Thoughts like these lead the wise king to cry despairingly, "Vanity of vanities!"—the first words of the book of Ecclesiastes. But Ecclesiastes ends on a very different note: "This is the end of the matter; all hath been heard; fear God and keep His commandments; for this is the whole duty of man." And the poet paints an inspiring picture of a divine vision, when the king becomes possessed of a faith that redeems from all evil and gives him back his lost happiness. It is said that this conclusion was added by the poet's father, or at the request of S. D. Luzzatto, who thus sacrificed the poetic conception on the altar of current public opinion.

The next Biblical poem demanding consideration is that entitled *Jael and Sisera*.

After his utter defeat by Barak and Deborah, Sisera flees from the battle, with Deborah in pursuit. He enters Jael's tent, begging shelter and water to quench his thirst. Jael recognises her people's persecutor (the Israelites and Kenites become a single nation in Lebensohn's poem), and plots his destruction. She gives him milk instead of water, and he, deeply touched, utters his thanks, blesses her and calls her an angel of salvation. Jael's face clouds over: the praise and blessing frighten her: she knows how little she deserves them. The poet skilfully describes the hard struggle that goes on in her kindly and honest heart. It is hard to harm one who has sought refuge in her tent; yet she is forced to it by her love for her people and country. Her guest, who has trusted her and put his life in her hands, and praised and blessed her—how can she kill him by stealth, while he sleeps and cannot defend himself? How can she be false to the law of hospitality, so sacred in the East, and turn deceitful and treacherous?

> Shall I draw sword against him who lies so securely, against a weary man slumbering so calmly and peacefully, knowing not that murder lies in wait for him? How sweet his sleep, how calm and restful! Perchance he even dreams of my kindly welcome. How terrible should he awake and see before him Jael with murderous weapons, unstable as water, treacherously cutting short his life, delivering him only in order to slay him: the same whom he had blessed, " As thine eyes took pity, so may the gracious God reward thee." Thus did he bless me, then laid him down to sleep; and maybe he blesses me now in spirit, while I—as he sleeps—take his life! To slay a man who has covenanted peace with me, when he is secure and unarmed, and tears of thankfulness are not yet dry on his face! Shall I repay those tears with blood, and stain peace with the blood of battle?

But suddenly she is seized with fierce hatred of her people's enemy and oppressor. How many of her kindred has he brought to the grave! How he has afflicted and crushed her people these twenty years! If he remains alive, he will certainly exact vengeance for his shameful defeat, and the blood of her people will again be poured out like water ..

> There sleeps the oppressor of my land, who forced thousands of my people to kneel before destruction, who reft the son from the mother's breast, and heard not her lament—why should not his mother be likewise bereft? Wherefore should this ruthless man sleep and live? Has he not robbed sleep from all eyes? When he awakens, will he not gather strength and power and crush my people with his heart of iron? And the blood of my people, alas, cries from the ground, " Fill thy hand, Jael, fill thy hand with vengeance!"

Then she invokes the Angel of Death*:

> Come, Murder, ascend from the deeps of destruction! Drive pity from my heart and all calm and graciousness! Fill my pure heart with venomous fury, set thy bloody cloak about me, take out the flesh of my heart and set therein a stone that will not hearken to laments nor understand entreaty! Set darkness over my eyes, that they see not what my hands do in this room; let thy venomous adders hiss, and lick the blood of this carcase in a moment!

And she takes up the hammer. But when she enters the tent where Sisera lies innocently sleeping, and hears him talking in his sleep

---
*cf. Shakespeare's *Macbeth* (Act I, Scene V).

and calling her an " angel from heaven,"
her doubts are stirred up afresh; but only for
a moment. Love for her people triumphs, and
before Sisera can awake from his sleep he
lies slain. But as he dies he is still able to
murmur :

> Jael, my angel art thou—the Angel of Death!

Jael hears and is terrified. The strong wave
of patriotic fervour has already passed away,
leaving her once more a simple, innocent
young woman, who cannot but be horrified at
the murder her own hands have committed.
She hears in the distance the happy shouting
of her people as they return from the battle-
field, crowned with victory. But she is far
from rejoicing :

> " Alas!" cried Jael, " this gladness is not
> mine; not my foeman have I slain, but him who
> took shelter with me."

She sees Deborah the Prophetess approaching
in " garment red," and the " sounds of
myriad voices roar like the sea," and she
hears them praising and blessing her name :

> Blessed above women shall Jael be,
> The wife of Heber the Kenite,
> Blessed shall she be above women in the
>   tent!

The eulogistic mention of her name in the inspired Song of Deborah gradually restores
her peace of mind : *vox populi vox Dei*—God
Himself blesses her work through the mouth
of prophetess and people. The people rejoice

—how then should not she rejoice?

Lebensohn sings us also the song of the tragic death of Judah Ha-Levi, the greatest of the Hebrew poets of the Middle Ages. The story is told that when he reached Jerusalem, the city which he had longed to see all his life, he fell on his face, kissed and embraced the dust of the Holy Land, and sang his immortal song, *Dost thou not ask, O Zion?*—then suddenly was slain by the sword of a brutal Arab trooper. Lebensohn describes Judah Ha-Levi as he waters the ground with his hot tears, in that holy land—

> In which every stone is an altar of the living God, each rock a platform for God's Prophet.

And he dreams of his great brethren who used to live in this land—the prophets and lawgivers, king David " the sweet singer of Israel," and Solomon, " wisest of all men." All these mighty dead gaze on him through their eye-sockets and stretch out their bony hands towards him. He falls into a trance, and at that very moment a living hand touches him, the hand of the brutal murderer. The dreaming poet, absorbed in his wonderful vision, cannot tell whether he feels the sharp edge of the sword in reality or only in his dream:

> The hands of the dead still touch him, his heart is still a-quiver from his dream, when suddenly—ah, shameful violence!—a living hand plunges the sword through his heart, and his blood gushes forth like torrents of water, and his

soul is swept away with the streaming blood. "Thou art become as we!" the dead cry.

A smile of pure joy—no fear of the shadow of death, but the glory of heavenly rapture—plays on his face; here his dream is ended—alas, for the death-bitter dream!—but the singer does not yet open his eyes.

For scarce did he slumber, weary and spent, when a cruel Arab, bold of front and hard of heart—brother to the leopard and friend of the adder—brought murder upon him in the evil fury of the sword.

Memory of his hallowed name will not end for Judah; when the pillaged daughter of Zion sorrows in the fast of the fifth month over the laments of the son of Hilkiah, her eyes weep over his song also.

Lebensohn's third volume, *Kinnor Bath Tziyon*, contains a large number of short poems, including many translations from Horace and Virgil, Schiller and Goethe, Mickiewicz, and Alfieri. Most of the original poems are about love and nature; in a few of them he bewails the gloomy fate that overshadowed his young life. The unfortunate poet wrote the best of his work as he lay on his death-bed in Berlin, far from his relations and friends. Like Heine, he sang from a "mattress grave," and most of his poems are fraught with bitter pain. Not that he was naturally melancholy or pessimistic. He did not wish for death: he loved life, thirsted and craved for it. But life was not for him:

Cursed be death, and life accurst!

he cries in the agony of his pain. How

keenly he loved pleasure, how passionately his emotions craved for satisfaction, we may see from his numerous love-poems. At once deep and tender, bitter and sweet, arrogant and bashful, they reveal in all its charm the lively and natural passion of a young heart. Here, for the first time in modern Hebrew literature, are love-poems worthy of the name, born not of imitation of European poets, but of a vivid and pulsing emotion. In the directness and spontaneity of his love-poems, Lebensohn not only surpasses all his predecessors and contemporaries in modern Hebrew literature. Even among our more recent poets there is perhaps none that can be compared with him except Tchernichovsky.

Among his poems there is one that is Zionist in subject-matter. The poet enquires of "The Forsaken Bough" that is ceaselessly tossed and hurled about by the waves of the sea, by stormy floods and tempests, and asks it where it comes from and why it can find no rest. The bough replies: "Because I was cut off from my native tree, from a verdant tree far off in the East, therefore do the stormy waters toss me about in endless unrest." Still earlier, in his introduction to *Songs of the Daughter of Zion* he says:
"Even though other masters now have the Holy Land in possession, it is still ours, for we have purchased its holy soil with rivers of blood and tears."

A friend of the younger and a pupil of the

elder Lebensohn was Judah Löb GORDON (1830-1892), one of the greatest Hebrew poets of all time. Like the younger Lebensohn, he chose for his earlier poems subjects from Jewish history. In 1857 appeared his *Love of David and Michal*, which is constructed on the lines of most historical poems, describing in twelve books the life and adventures of David, king of Israel. It betrays the influence of Schiller and also of the two Lebensohns. In construction and artistic finish it is much inferior to the poetry of the younger Lebensohn. It lacks the other's passion and poetical facility. On the other hand, it is rich in ideas new to that generation. Gordon's style, however, lacks the younger Lebensohn's brilliant colours and bold and passionate imagery. Despite the abundant emotional power that marks all Gordon's poetry, he cannot be reckoned a great lyric poet. His love-poems and nature-poems are not original in imagery nor spontaneous in feeling, nor do they rise to great poetic heights. But Gordon had emotional gifts that were all his own, combined with considerable psychological insight and an unlimited command of Hebrew. Thus he excels in the clearness and precision of his style, especially in the imaginative handling of philosophical problems, and in the poetic expression of the finer shades of meaning. Here he surpasses the younger and even the elder Lebensohn. The *Maskilim* of those days had not yet learnt to appreciate poetry æsthetically. What they looked for in poetry was not artistic creation, the worth and beauty of which they could neither understand nor appreciate; it was rather a kind of lyrical philosophy that appealed both to their understanding and to their emotions. Hence it is not surprising that Gordon very soon attracted the attention of the reading public far more than did the younger Lebensohn.

In the eighteen-fifties Gordon wrote a few love-poems which are marked more by *melitzah* and poetical philosophising than by simple emotion, and also a fine rhymed idyll, entitled *David and Barzillai*.

When David fled from his son, Absalom, and came to Mahanaim, a rich old farmer from Rogelim, Barzillai the Gileadite, brought the king "beds and basons and earthern vessels" and provision for his army, "wheat and barley and meal and parched corn" and the like. When Absalom was killed and David was returning to Jerusalem, he proposed to Barzillai that he should come with him and spend his remaining days in the king's court, in pleasure and luxury. But the old farmer, who had toiled on the land from childhood, refused the king's proposal: a field filled with God's blessing was more to him than all the pleasures of a king's court; he preferred his flocks and trees and flowers to the noisy pageant of court life. He draws the king a picture of the unrest and hurry of town life, particularly life in the capital, with its foul air, its false glamour and its artificial pleasures, behind which lurk unhappiness and anxiety:

> For those who pluck the harp-strings weep in secret, and much sorrow dwelleth in fine houses; rivers of tears run over the golden dust, and behind all desire lurks loathing and the grave.

The king is amazed at what he hears: he stands "like a pillar of marble set up by the craftsman," sunk in thought. Is not the old farmer right? Is not a quiet, peaceful life, the simple, honest life of the peasant, far better in reality than the life of him who wields the royal sceptre? Are royal pleasures worth the care and trouble they entail? The idea, of course, is not by any means new; but Gordon endowed the ancient Hebrew rural life with such graceful charm that its primitive simplicity captured the hearts of the least romantic.

Gordon, like the younger Lebensohn, was moved to treat of such subjects by an intense interest in that distant past in which Hebrew was still a spoken language. This interest the *Maskilim* of that period derived on the historical side from Rapoport, Krochmal and Luzzatto, and on the linguistic side from the *Ha-Meassef* group of writers and their followers in Galicia and Russia. But Gordon was further influenced by a desire to popularise the idea of agriculture among his people: for at that time, in the reign of

Nicholas I, the Russian government and many of the intellectual leaders of Jewry were attempting to propagate this idea among the Jews (it was about this time that Jewish agricultural settlements were established in the Kherson, Ekaterinoslav and Vilna districts). These two incentives, and particularly the first, also produced the first novel in modern Hebrew literature.

By that time, namely, the early 'fifties, most departments of literature were represented in modern Hebrew. It had its educational propagandists (Günzburg, Erter, Isaac Bär Levinsohn), and its scholars (Rapoport, Krochmal, Luzzatto); it also had a wealth of lyric and other poetry (Wessely, Letteris, the two Lebensohns, and Gordon). Hebrew literature lacked only an original school of novelists. It was Abraham MAPU (1808-1868) who first filled this gap.

Mapu had an unusually rich imagination and a lively and emotional temperament. Few knew the Scriptures, or, rather, felt them, as he did—their spirit, their stately oriental beauty, and the secret of the living history that wells up from them so vigorously. As he meditated on the books of the Prophets, Mapu's spirit was transported to ancient times. He breathed the atmosphere of ancient Judæa in the days of Hezekiah, king of Judah, and Isaiah, the son of Amoz; and he can transport us also to the same distant past. His novel, "The Love of Zion" (*Ahavath*

Tziyon, Vilna, 1853) marks a new epoch in Hebrew literature. Mapu did not merely describe that ancient epoch in the usual manner of the historical novelist: he lived within himself the life of the Zion of Bible times, and described that life like a contemporary and an eye-witness. In reading the novel, it is almost impossible to escape the feeling that we have here a work written 2,500 years ago by one of the Prophets, or by the poet of the Song of Songs, or by the author of the Book of Ruth.

The plot of the novel is complicated and artificial, and at the same time naive almost to the point of puerility. Its leading figures are of the type that is found in the eighteenth-century French pastoral romances, with a certain admixture of Eugène Sue and the elder Dumas. Yet this does not detract from the value of the novel as a whole. The reader marvels at the inner illumination, the veritable "holy spirit" by which Mapu's insight has succeeded in penetrating the innermost life of the time, a life so distant and different from the life of his day. No historian or archæologist specialising in the period could show us so realistically as Mapu the life of Judæa and Samaria, with their true prophets and their false prophets, their kings and priests, masters and servants, their customs and their manners, their conversation and affairs, and their winding processions and moving crowds. Yet with Mapu it is all as simple and natural as in the Bible itself. And with it all he is so lucid and interesting that the reader feels the big, uncomplicated life rustling by him as on some day in the time of Isaiah and Hezekiah—that unique manner of life, so rich in great men, the teachers of the human race, veritable pillars of the world, yet at the same time utterly simple and primitive: a life at once so small and so large.

The impression which *Ahavath Tziyon* made on its Hebrew readers was immense. For the Russian Jew of the 'fifties, this work, besides the qualities that we have enumerated, had a quite special appeal. The Ghetto Jew, with his spiritual horizon bounded by arid religious routine, was suddenly confronted with a picture of a new life, untrammelled, youthful, exuberant, with no trace of Ghetto or subjection or servitude, no merely mechanical religious ceremonial; and this life was the life of his own people, that genuine Hebrew life which had given to the Jewish people and to humanity the most precious gifts of the spirit, had given the prophets themselves, the very Isaiah who appeared in Mapu's pages as a living and active hero. The young Jew, who had hitherto thought of the kings and Prophets of Israel as occupied only with religious matters, found in this glorious past, re-created for him by Mapu, the ideal of national freedom which his people had lost in the Dark Ages. Thus this novel became a sort of stepping-stone to the Zionist idea.

The Jewish heart was stirred to new life. The luxuriant scenery of the East; Jerusalem's intoxicating beauty; the joy of harvest and vintage; the pure, artless love of Tamar, daughter of Jedidiah the Judæan nobleman, for the shepherd Amnon, who had saved her from the lion's jaws; her brother Teman's burning love for Peninah the reaper; and, finally, the great motley crowds which, at the " Three Feasts," came thronging up to Jerusalem from all parts of the land of Israel—what a pageant of joy and magic for the young Jew, who had never known anything before except the tractates of the Talmud and the hair-splitting casuistries of the rabbinical commentators! Thus it came about that Mapu's novel did more to spread *Haskalah* among the frequenters of the rabbinical seminaries than hundreds of volumes that directly preached the doctrines of " enlightenment."

Ahavath Tziyon had yet another quality of inestimable value. The Prophets had risen in revolt against the pretensions of charlatans and hypocrites. " To what purpose is the multitude of your sacrifices unto me? saith the Lord . . . your hands are full of blood." Such is the substance of many chapters in the book of Isaiah. Thus Chapter 58 denounces the fastings in which the ungodly " bow down their heads like a rush " at the very time when they call " for strife and contention " and " smite with the fist of wickedness." To them the Prophet says, " Is not this the fast that I have chosen? to loose the bonds of wickedness . . . to let the oppressed go free," " to deal thy bread to the hungry and that thou bring the poor that are cast out to thy house; when thou seest the naked, that thou cover him, and that thou hide not thyself from thine own flesh?"

These ideas are the background both of *Ahavath Tziyon* and of Mapu's second and longer novel, *Ashmath Shomeron*, " The Sin of Samaria " (1865). The latter deals with the same period, and contains descriptions drawn with even greater art than those in *Ahavath Tziyon*; but its plot is hopelessly confused, and its characters are so numerous that they pass before the reader like shadows and fail to leave the necessary impression. In these two novels Mapu depicts the hostility of the true prophets to the priests and the false prophets (more particularly to the priests, whom the true prophets condemned because they urged the multiplication of sacrifices even though they were offered without true religious intention, and thus laid all the stress on routine observance). Priests and false prophets alike appear as deceivers and hypocrites, who make outward observance of religious forms a cloak for their evil practices and offences against the moral law, which is the sovereign principle in the eyes of God and His prophets. Thus these ancient hypocrites were made to represent the religious humbugs of Mapu's own day. Zimri, who appears as the villain in both novels, is shown as the archetype of all charlatans and hypocrites, and not only of those who were contemporary with Isaiah and Hezekiah. Through the thin, transparent, historical wrapping it is easy to see that Mapu was not castigating the ancient Zimris so much as the charlatans and hypocrites of his own time, who also rated the externals of religion and the conventional lies of stereotyped tradition more highly than loving-kindness and sincere piety. This explains why Mapu and all his readers were the target for persecution by the more bigoted among the orthodox, although at first sight there would seem to be no harm in the historical subject-matter of the books, and although the orthodox themselves profess to hold the Prophets in great veneration. The forces of obscurantism realised that the Prophets as painted by Mapu were a source of light—and darkness dreads the light. The orthodox saw that the false prophets and hypocrites, the Mattans, Zimris and Pashhurs and their like, could serve as a mirror from which their own degraded image was reflected; and they felt also that soon Mapu would not rest content with historical types only, but would pass on to the life of his own time, and the bigots of Kovno would replace the bigots of Jerusalem.

Hence to read *Ahavath Tziyon* was, in the eyes of the Jewish orthodoxy of the time, as bad as to read heretical writings—a fact which rather increased than diminished the number of Mapu's readers.

CHAPTER III
THE PERIOD OF REALISM

In the 'sixties of last century, a noticeable change took place in Hebrew literature: Romanticism gave place to Realism. Till that time, from *Shire Tif'ereth* to *David and Barzillai*, *Ahavath Tziyon* and *Ashmath Shomeron*, it had been full of longing for the past, exaggerated emotionalism and panegyrics to "heaven-sent enlightenment." From the 'sixties onwards it turned its attention to the present, to actual life, to the concrete needs of society, state and nation.

There was still another change. Hebrew writers had hitherto fought only on the defensive against religious prejudices and the old manner of Jewish life. Henceforward, until the 'eighties, they took the offensive. Günzburg and the two Lebensohns had only claimed toleration for modern learning: they dared not touch openly on the root problems of Jewish life, which was so bound up with the complicated and burdensome laws of the Talmud. Even Mapu at first only dared to hint at the petrified state of the Jewish faith and the hypocrisy of its official representatives. Then came a radical change in the course of modern Hebrew literature. Whether this was a consequence of internal development within Russian Judaism itself, or whether it was due to the influence of the new movement in Russian literature during the 'sixties, or whether, as is more likely, it was a result of both, in any case the fact is that at this time Mapu, the Romantic of Romantics, who had sought refuge from the painful present in the poetic past of Isaiah and Hezekiah, began to publish his great novel, "The Painted Hawk" (*'Ait Tzavu'a*, 1857-1861), the purpose of which was a realistic portrayal of the gloomy present. The characters in this novel are contemporary types in the strictest sense. The leading character, the pietist Rabbi Zadok, whose deceit and cunning are excessive even for a veritable Tartuffe; the orthodox and jesuitical Rabbi Gadiel, who thunders against all readers of heretical books (such as, for example, *Ahavath Tziyon*); the simple-minded believer, old Obadiah, tricked and exploited by Rabbi Zadok and Rabbi Gadiel, whom he regards as saints; the illiterate, superstitious and tyrannical Gaal, who has risen by unscrupulous means from the gutter to wealth and high position, and whose religion serves him as a means of getting riches and honour; Jerahmeel, the classical example of the *Batlan* (i.e., the naive, harmless Talmud student, knowing nothing of the world and simple to the point of imbecility); Nahshon, the classical type of the marriage-broker, subtle and full of tricks, who sees and knows everything, a great expert in the Talmud and its expounders, whose wise saws he scatters right and left, and with an endless stream of "great ideas"—these were living and characteristic Jewish types in the 'fifties and 'sixties, and are very skilfully described by Mapu in his third novel, *The Painted Hawk*. Few of his successors have so successfully presented such vivid and distinctive types as the Obadiahs, Jerahmeels and Nahshons of Mapu. All the moral degradation lurking behind the mask of religion, all the poverty of mind concealed by sham erudition, all the futile casuistry, all the narrow-mindedness and petrifaction of the Judaism of that time are graphically portrayed with artistic verisimilitude. The story of *The Painted Hawk*, too, is full of such natural and lively humour that the enormous effect which it produced in its day can be readily understood. The Hebrew reader of that generation had no artistic standards, and did not stop to notice how unnatural was the sequence of events in the story, and how full of fantastic and abnormal incidents; nor did he realise that the moral turpitude of the bad characters (Zadok, Gadiel, etc.) was over-emphasised, while the good characters (the agriculturists like Naaman, and the feminine devotees of *Haskalah* like Elizabeth and Athaliah) were mere lay figures, with no initiative or clearly-marked individuality. These modernist young men and women make long, flowery speeches about the value of " heaven-sent enlightenment "—and the youth of that time demanded nothing more. What was essential was to make a breach in the great Chinese wall which hemmed in Jewish life, and to give the young generation the ability to see that beyond the breach was a richer and more colourful world. This Mapu achieved in his last novel.

It has already been mentioned that the elder Lebensohn's allegorical play, *Truth and Faith*, appeared in 1866. Its hero, Zibeon, differs but little in his main features from the hypocritical Rabbi Zadok. The long conversations on genuine religion—which in the author's view goes hand in hand with " enlightenment," as contrasted with the Ghetto religion, which is befogged with illusions and superstitions—made, as might be expected, a very strong impression on the young Talmudical students; and Lebensohn's drama served as a complement to Mapu's novel.

In 1868 appeared a new novel on contemporary Jewish life—*Fathers and Sons*, by Shalom Jacob ABRAMOVITZ (1834-1918), afterwards famous under the pseudonym " Mendelé Mocher Sefarim " (Mendelé the Bookseller), of whom more will be said in a later chapter. This novel closely resembles *The Painted Hawk*, but there is a difference : Mapu described the life of the Jews of Lithuania, while Abramovitz described that of the Hasidic Jews of Volhynia. Also, Abramovitz was the first to introduce into modern Hebrew literature a sort of new Hebrew jargon, made up of Talmudic expressions and literal translations of Yiddish sentences, which enabled him successfully to imitate the simple speech of the Jewish masses. Thanks to this idiom, the conversations of his characters are like the actual talk of living men and women. The novel was so highly esteemed that it was translated into Russian by J. L. Bienstock from the manuscript, and was published in Russian before the Hebrew original appeared in print.

Abramovitz had already begun to publish a "Natural History" in Hebrew. Natural science, because it deals with material reality, was popular with Russian writers in the 'sixties; and this work on natural history was an attempt to give some real education to the Hebrew-reading public, whose writers had till then merely talked about *Haskalah*. This notable work, in three volumes, contains, besides scientific information in popular form, a full vocabulary of names, partly invented and partly based on the terminology of the Talmud and other early writings, for those beasts and birds which had had no names, or no definitely accepted names, in Hebrew. Abramovitz thus not only gave the Hebrew reader the opportunity of studying an important branch of knowledge in a familiar language, but also enriched modern Hebrew with a large number of very necessary words.

A great deal more was done for popular education by Kalman SCHULMAN (1819-1899). He compiled a *History of the World* in nine volumes (1867-1884) (based on the German work by Weber) and a *Geography* in ten volumes (1871-1877); and in 1857-1860 he translated Eugène Sue's *Mystères de Paris*, which the younger generation swallowed with avidity. He also compiled a *History of Jewish Scholars* of the Spanish period, 1872-1879 (based on Graetz), and he translated almost the whole of the works of Josephus. He wrote several books on Jewish antiquities (*Ways of Old*, 1854; *Shulamith*, 1855; *The Rose of Sharon*, 1861; *The Treasury*, 1880, etc.), which manifest great love and veneration for Palestine. In addition, he translated many articles on nature-study and general history. His pure Biblical Hebrew, though flowery and archaic and inexact, fell gratefully on the ears of his young Jewish readers by reason of its easy flow, its emotional quality, and its Old Testament charm. Shulman thus did much to inspire affection for the ancient yet ever-young national language, and for the ancestral land which, even in its desolate state, retained its own peculiar fascination.

In 1865 and the following years there appeared the first serious attempts at literary criticism in Hebrew. Uri KOVNER (1842-1909) published two pamphlets, *Heker Davar* (1865) and *Tzeror Perahim* (1868), which caused a sensation at the time. Abraham PAPERNA (1840-1919) wrote his critical pamphlet, *Old wine in new bottles*, in 1868, and in the same year appeared a pamphlet entitled *Let there be criticism* (*Bikkoreth Tihyeh*) by Peretz SMOLENSKIN (1842-1885), about whom we shall have more to say in the next chapter.

Ten years earlier (1856) began the first Hebrew weekly periodical, *Ha-Maggid*, edited in Lück, East Prussia, by a Russian Jew, Eliezer SILBERMANN. It contained political and general news, news-correspondence from all quarters of Jewry, and articles dealing with Jewish social problems. It had also a literary section, which included poetry and articles of scholarly and scientific interest, both Jewish and general. The existence of a weekly paper, issued with the regularity and in the form of periodicals written in living languages, helped materially to develop Hebrew literature and to increase the number of its regular readers. *Ha-Maggid* served also as a rallying-point for Jews of all countries. It had contributors as well as readers everywhere. Jewish scholars in Germany and Russia, in Austria and Italy, in India and Turkey, all alike contributed to this Hebrew periodical, which, through its use of the national language, united Jews the world over. But it had one fundamental defect: in its attempt to secure the largest possible circulation it tried to please all sections of Jewry. By this means it certainly increased the number of Hebrew readers; but in order to avoid making enemies it had to include all the new ideas and points of view that began to germinate in Russian Jewry during its early years. Shortly afterwards two other Hebrew weeklies appeared : *Ha-Carmel* (with a Russian supplement, 1860-1870; it was later converted into a monthly, 1871-1880), edited in Vilna by the historian Samuel Joseph FUENN (1818-1890), and *Ha-Melitz*, edited in Odessa by Alexander ZEDERBAUM (1816-1893). Some time afterwards, *Ha-Tzefirah* was produced by Hayyim Selig SLONIMSKY (1810-1904), a mathematician and author of several Hebrew works on algebra, geometry and astronomy. *Ha-Carmel* was of even less living interest than *Ha-Maggid*; in its attitude towards new and independent ideas it was not radically different (only in the field of Jewish scholarship was its contribution of importance), and it did not long survive. *Ha-Tzefirah* at first confined itself to literary and scientific subjects, and, until the 'eighties, did not deal with current problems. *Ha-Melitz* (1860-1903) became the mouthpiece of the best Hebrew writers and the channel of the fresh ideas that were simmering in the Jewish world of the latter half of the 19th century. It provided a platform for the two greatest champions of *Haskalah* and freedom of thought, the propagandist Moses Löb LILIENBLUM (1843-1910) and the poet Judah Löb

Gordon (already mentioned in the preceding chapter), with their demand for more or less far-reaching reforms in the *Shulhan Arukh* and the education of the new generation. Lilienblum's ideas, as expressed in his article "Talmud Paths" (1868) and other articles published in *Ha-Melitz* from 1868 to 1870, may be summed up as follows.

The *Shulhan Arukh* is a product of the Ghetto, and with the dawn of a new and free life it is no longer a satisfactory guide. Its stringency exceeds that of its original source, the Talmud; in recent centuries the Rabbis have turned away from the spirit of the Talmud, which has underlying it the idea of progress and adaptation to the changing conditions of life. The Talmud contains many progressive ideas, and even shows a leaning towards reform; but these ideas, owing to the incessant persecutions of the Middle Ages, have failed to develop and materialise in Jewish religious life. The Rabbis of the Talmud modified any religious ordinance which, through change of circumstances, had become too burdensome to be generally observed; in all their enactments they had regard to the condition and the needs of the people. But for the last thousand years these requirements have been disregarded: this was an inevitable result of the narrow and isolated Ghetto life. Now, however, when the Ghetto walls have been broken down, the time has come to purify the Jewish faith of

the accumulated dross of the Middle Ages—
of all those accretions which prevent the
people from finding satisfaction for their
most essential needs. Such was the demand which Lilienblum
presented to the Rabbis in a series of striking
articles, based on an expert's knowledge of
the Talmud and the later religious literature. At the same time Gordon also forsook
the dead past and his love-poems. At the
call of Lilienblum he joined in the struggle
against ignorance and superstition, and
wrote a number of polemical and controversial pieces of great satirical power and
critical acumen.

These articles aroused the ire of the anti-modernists, who fought these new "heretics"
tooth and nail. Lilienblum was living at the
time in Vilkomir, a small provincial town in
Lithuania, and so great was the persecution
to which he was subjected by the ultra-conservative elements, that he was forced to
leave and settle in Odessa (1870). Here he
began his literary career as a member of the
staff of *Ha-Melitz*, and later he became a contributor to *Ha-Shahar*, a journal published
in Vienna from 1869 to 1884 (with intermissions) and edited by Peretz Smolenskin. In
1872 he contributed to *Ha-Shahar* a long review of Mapu's *Painted Hawk*, entitled "A
World of Chaos," and written in the spirit
of the Russian critic, Pisareff, then a great
influence in Russian literature. Charges of

lack of utilitarian aim against great writers and poets like Poushkin were then fashionable, and the criticism of Mapu from this standpoint made a strong impression. This partially explains why the author of *The Love of David and Michal*, after becoming acquainted with the work of the Russian author Nekrasov, turned his attention to current problems.

The influence of Pisareff and Tschernishefsky is specially noticeable in Lilienblum's *The Sins of Youth* (1876). Hardly a single problem of Jewish life and religion is left untouched in this book, a book which remains unique in subject and style. With a simplicity and self-revelation equal to that of Rousseau, Lilienblum writes the " Confessions " of a Talmudical Jew of the 'sixties. He opens out his heart without reserve, lays bare his innermost thoughts and feelings, reveals his religious struggles, and all the travail of a fresh young soul that had been awakened to new life; and all this with simple directness and extraordinary clarity. The book includes a number of letters which are of value as human documents. It reflects clearly and faithfully the ardent, restless spirit of the best *maskilim* of the time, who had suddenly come out of darkness into light, or rather into twilight, and had not yet found the right path. They saw that the older Judaism, on whose altar they had sacrificed their youth, was out of date; yet to abandon it altogether or to create a new Judaism was beyond their power: they were not ready for it, nor was there any solid ground on which to build anew. Pisareff's realism was not the only element that penetrated modern Hebrew literature. In 1876 the first Hebrew socialist proclamation appeared in London, and the next year the monthly journal *Ha-Emeth* ("The Truth"), with pronounced socialist tendencies, was founded by a group of Hebrew socialists led by A. FRIEMANN-LIEBERMANN (who wrote under the pen-name "BAR-DERORA"). It did not survive for long: Hebrew readers were not ready for its ideas, and the censorship would not suffer it to enter Russia, where most Hebrew readers were to be found. But a socialistic tendency could be discerned in much that appeared in *Ha-Shahar*, particularly in the poems of Judah Löb LEWIN; and when the weekly newspaper *Ha-Kol* appeared, in 1878, the Hebrew socialists contributed articles and feuilletons to its columns and more especially to its monthly supplement, "The Assembly of Sages." Among its contributors were "BEN-NETZ" (M. Winchefsky) and others, who afterwards used Yiddish as their propagandist medium, and in it also appeared Lilienblum's *The Teaching of Elisha ben Abuyah*, which deals with labour and feminist problems in the spirit of Russian socialism of the 'seventies, and views literature and science from the standpoint of "historical materialism."

Lilienblum's views on the need for religious reform also found expression in Hebrew belles-lettres. In 1877, in the new Hebrew monthly *Ha-Boker Or* ("Light at Morning Time"), published in Lemberg by the poet Abraham Baer GOTTLOBER (1814-1899)—a poet of the head rather than of the heart—there began to appear a novel entitled *Religion and Life*, by Reuben Asher BRAUDES (1851-1902), one of the best of modern Hebrew novelists. The hero, Samuel, destined to be a Rabbi, fights in the cause of the Talmud and its principles of adjustability and progress against excessive and oppressive religious stringency; in other words, against the *Shulhan Arukh* and its commentators. This novel is one of the most important works of the period of militant *Haskalah*. Lilienblum's ideas, and all the miseries and persecutions which they brought upon him, here take shape in an artistic presentation sometimes reminiscent of Spielhagen's *In Reih' und Glied*. Such stories heartened the younger generation in their struggle against superstitious conservatism.

This struggle had already produced a number of propagandists and novelists, but it still awaited a great poet to invest it with emotional fire. He, too, was not long in coming; from the 'sixties onwards Gordon's poems became more and more concerned with current social problems.

In 1860 Gordon published a collection of fables for the young, entitled *Mishlé Yehudah*, which included, along with translations from Lafontaine, Kryloff and others, a few original fables of great merit. Both the translated and the original fables are so remarkable for their classical Hebrew style that even the Karaites made use of them in the elementary reading-books used in their schools.

In 1868 Gordon published a collection of poems, *Songs of Judah*, afterwards included in the first and third volumes of his collected works. Some of these poems belong to his earlier romantic period, as, for example, *Asenath, Daughter of Potiphera*, which is based on an old tradition to the effect that Joseph married the daughter of Potiphar's wife, Zuleika, whose advances he had resisted. The poet describes the slave Joseph's chaste love for his master's beautiful daughter, Asenath. She returns his love, and when Zuleika charges Joseph with attempting her virtue, and Joseph is put in prison, the daughter is torn between her implicit faith in the truthfulness of her mother, whom she esteems as a good daughter should, and her love for Joseph, which will not suffer her to doubt his love and constancy. It is she, according to the poet's invention, who, after she has been made one of the ladies of the queen of Egypt's court, reminds Pharaoh of the wise slave now enchained in the prison dungeon. Thus it is by the power and might of love that Joseph becomes ruler of all the land of Egypt and husband of his faithful and devoted Asenath, the daughter of his bitter enemy, Zuleika. The description of the luxurious Egyptian scenery and the account of the elaborate Egyptian ceremonial lend a special charm to this pleasing poem.

Far more remarkable is Gordon's well-known poem *In the Depths of the Sea*. Here he describes the expulsion from Spain in 1492 in lines of passionate protest:

> The daughter of Jacob was exiled utterly from Spain; reaching the gates of Gaul she was likewise thrust thence; Europe turned its back upon the dispersed wanderers, and only the grave stood yawning before them, nothing but Tophet and destruction. They left their bones on the rocks of Africa, and their blood was spilt in Asia; seas became dry with the weight of corpses, and on land streams of blood flowed like water. And the judge of the world remained shut in his dark secret place, and the tears of the oppressed were not avenged beneath the heavens.
>
> Out of the books and chronicles my ear hearkens to the cry of those who are dragged away to the slaughter, the voice of captives suffering in dungeons and at the block, the graves of the beaten and afflicted with their outpoured blood; the cry of martyrs tortured on the rack and burnt alive at the stake; the voice of Jacob walking in misery and anguish, pursued down the long avenue of generations, and trampled in the dust, each age increasing his troubles and renewing his old

wounds; Crusades, Disputations of Faith and Wars of Religion.

The story told in the poem is simple. The expelled Jews sail from Spain to Africa, where they hope to find a temporary refuge. Among them are two women, the wife of the Rabbi of Tortona, Abu Shaam, who has been burnt by the Inquisition, and his beautiful daughter Peninah. The captain of the ship casts his eyes on Peninah, and threatens that unless she yields to him he will land all the Jews in the ship on a desert island and leave them to die of hunger and thirst. The girl's heart is torn by an inner conflict. Finally she decides to save her poor brethren, but at the cost not of her honour but of her life; and in this resolution she is supported by her mother. The Jews are saved. They all disembark, and only the two women remain on board.

> And as the dawn rises to drive back the night, so the two valiant women rose as lionesses, paced with unfaltering step to the side of the ship, and with rent and seething hearts poured out their prayer:
>
> "One only Lord, O Lord our God, behold us, who have come to thee; pray receive us! If our blood be sweet to thee as a sacrifice, we perish as a free-will offering upon thine altar!"
>
> They spoke and raised their eyes to heaven . . . and slipped from the ship's deck into the water. . . .

That is the end of the story. But the poet

cannot contain himself, and he continues :

> The sea beheld, and fled in terror, its waves roared and surged round about; and the two souls, pure as gold, sank to the watery depths like lead. There they ceased from turmoil, there 'mid the roots of the mountains they found rest: the rocks their monument and the sea's bosom their grave, their dome the firmament and their epitaph the stars. There was none to see or weep for their misfortune. Only the eyelids of the dawn were opened wide for them, only the Eye of Earth gazed silently at the clouds—the Eye that sees the end of all flesh, the end of untold thousands, yet has never dropped a tear.

This poem, like *Asenath, Daughter of Potiphera*, has no real connection with the *Haskalah* campaign which dominated that period. Another poem, *In the Lion's Jaws*, reveals the new tendency of Gordon's muse. This poem depicts the siege of Jerusalem by Titus, and the poet uses this episode to attack the early Rabbis of the Talmud, who advocated peace with Rome, because for them the study of the Law was the primary essential for the Jews, and they were wholly indifferent (according to Gordon) to the nation's political servitude and the degraded condition of the masses :

> They have destroyed thee, O Israel, for they have not taught thee to wage war with skill and knowledge. What can strength and bitterness of spirit avail thee if there is no leader to plan, if there is no discipline? For centuries thy teachers have directed thee, building houses of study: and

what have they taught thee? They have taught thee to tend the wind, to plough the stone, to draw water in a sieve, to thresh straw. They have taught thee, alas, to go against life, to shut thyself up alone within fences and walls, to be dead on earth and alive in heaven, to dream awake and speak in visions. And so thy sap is gone, thy spirit is enfeebled, thy heart is troubled, thy strength is dried up. They have battened thee with the dust of scribes and musty tomes, and have set thee before the world like a living mummy.

Such violent abuse of the early Jewish religious teachers was a thing unheard-of in modern Hebrew poetry until the 'seventies of last century. Nor was it in the slightest degree relevant to the subject of the poem. But at this period Gordon was so obsessed by the struggle for *Haskalah* that he could not refrain from attacking orthodoxy even in a poem on a purely historical subject. However, even if we strip the poem of these striking irrelevancies, it still remains a poetical work of outstanding quality, artistically superior to all Gordon's other historical poems. Its principal character is Simon Bar Giora, one of the leaders in the war for the liberation of Jerusalem from Titus. The wound which he had received in a previous battle is still unhealed; he is in love with the tender Martha, and finds it hard to part from her —perhaps for ever; but he hastens to the field of battle, to fight for his oppressed country's freedom, and Martha herself girds his sword around him :

"Go, Simon my beloved, go lead thine army! Each moment is more precious than gold: haste away! The eyes of our country are upon thee; have no thought of me—there is no need. I have seen my father and my brother struck dead, and all the horrors of death I know. The day wanes, the shades of evening fall—hark to the cries of the oppressor! Every heart trembles. I will gird thy weapons about thee: here is thy sword, the sword of God and our country!"

She spake, and her face was aflame, and the tears welled from her eyes. For a few moments they embraced, clasped heart to heart, and passionately kissed. "Farewell, Martha, delight of my eyes!"

"Fare thee well, Simon, till the heavens are no more." And heart-broken the young warrior tore himself away and went down to the gate for life or death.

But Israel's warriors, in spite of their unique courage and heroism, which amazed even the hardened Romans, cannot withstand the Roman legions, and Simon is taken captive. Titus, the *deliciæ generis humani* of Tacitus, arranges a gladiatorial show in the circus at Rome, in which Simon is forced to fight with a Libyan lion. Martha has been sold as a slave to a Roman matron, and is forced to accompany her mistress to this cruel spectacle, doubly horrible to her. As soon as she looks at the ring, she recognises her beloved hero among those destined to be the lion's prey. He, however, intent on his fight with the lion, does not notice her at first. He summons up his remaining strength and drives his sword into the lion's side; but the sword is broken by the iron ribs of the king of beasts . . . And as he stands stupefied and crushed amid the icy waves of dumb despair, the hilt of his broken sword in his hand, and his glances wandering in search of help and pity, but finding nothing but " stony hearts around," there flashes on him, out of the crowd, the face of Martha. Her look of deep distress and boundless love gives him fresh heart and strength, and he would emulate the heroic Samson, who seized the lion and " rent him as he would have rent a kid," but " the God of Samson turned aside from his people and his warriors and was with the uncircumcised Philistines." So Martha sees the lion trample down her lover and tear him in pieces. And at the same moment that the soul left the warrior's body, mangled " in the lion's jaws," his beloved's soul also forsook this vale of weeping. The tragedy of this moving spectacle leaves an ineffaceable impression on the reader.

Some time afterwards, in 1879, Gordon wrote his poem, or rather, monologue, *Zedekiah in Prison*. We have seen how Gordon attacked the Sages of the Talmud in his *In the Lion's Jaws*. He went much further in *Zedekiah in Prison*. Like the Jewish religious teachers in the time of Titus, the prophet Jeremiah in the time of Nebuchadnezzar opposed the war of Jewish independence. Zedekiah, once king of Judah, has been defeated in battle, his sons have been slaughtered before his eyes by Nebuchadnezzar's order, and the Chaldeans have put out his eyes and imprisoned him for the rest of his life. The unhappy king cries out against Providence, and condemns the Prophets, first for their excessive devotion to an abstract and spiritual Judaism, which hampers the political and economic development of the Jewish nation, and secondly for their greed of power and their efforts to bend the kings of Israel and Judah to their will. Zedekiah recalls the struggle between the prophet Samuel and king Saul, which brought Saul to madness and ruin. In lines of unsurpassable vigour and incisiveness the poet sets forth the doctrine of theocracy and shows that it must be fought in the name of cultural progress. Then follow melancholy reflections on the lot of the Jewish people, interspersed with bitter complaints at the personal sufferings of Zedekiah. Thanks to its consummate artistry, the poem has lost nothing of its value by the flight of time. Through the thin disguise of the struggle against the old theocratic system, it is easy to discern the bitter struggle of Gordon's own time, between the orthodox Rabbis and the *Maskilim*. Many of the ideas about the excessive otherworldliness of the Prophets and their negation of the life of this world, which were afterwards elaborated by Renan and

Nietzsche, already find clear expression in this noteworthy poem.

As early as 1871 Gordon had begun to contribute to *Ha-Shahar* a series of poems quite obviously directed against the orthodox rabbis and the petrified religious system for which they stood. To that year belong his *Little Fables for Grown-up Children*, a collection of satirical poems remarkable alike for their matter and their form. In a very popular and lively style Gordon makes mock of the hypocrites and those who sacrifice their lives for the sake of the dead letter. Soon after, also in *Ha-Shahar*, appeared *Asaka D'rispak* ("On the shaft of a litter"), of which the subject-matter was novel and the censorious intention very obvious.

The plot of this poem is as follows: Eliphelet is a poverty-stricken carter, who makes the barest of livings by hard and unremitting toil. Before the Passover he works doubly hard to provide what is needed for the feast of unleavened bread, "wherein shall no leaven be seen"; and, thanks be to God, all goes well: Eliphelet has the necessary unleavened cakes, also wine enough for the "four cups" and meat in honour of the festival. But, alas! earthly happiness is short-lived. His wife, Sarah, finds a grain of barley in the soup; and then, horror of horrors, yet another grain; and there he is, with "leaven at Passover"! Eliphelet, being a common man, does not see any necessity to consult a rabbi about the grains of barley: he feels that from the rabbis he may expect only the worst—for the soup, the meat, and all the Passover utensils. But Sarah is more scrupulous: she hurries off to the rabbi's house with the question, "Is soup proper to be eaten after two grains of barley have been found in it?" The rabbi rules that the soup may not be used for food or profit; what is worse, he prohibits the use of all the vessels in which the Passover food has been prepared. For the poor woman this is a terrible misfortune; but worse is in store. Her husband, who had no wish to get the rabbi's opinion, conceives a dislike for his wife, who has disregarded him and gone off to the rabbi, and things reach such a pitch that the husband, although he has long lived peacefully and happily with his wife, divorces her. Thus for two grains of barley the rabbi has destroyed two souls; and all because of some inane rule out of the *Shulhan Arukh*!

In Gordon's most famous poem, *The Point of a Yod*, the heroine loses happiness because of another rule, or rather, because of nothing more than a single letter, "the point of a *yod*," of a jot or tittle that was matter for doubt.

The beautiful Bath-Shua is married to a feeble, unmanly, fifteen-year-old youth who has never learnt anything but Talmud; she had never seen him before marriage, and she becomes his wife merely because his great knowledge of the Talmud and the rabbinical commentaries has won her father's admiration. The pitiful life to which the Jewish woman was condemned in the rigidly orthodox, patriarchal Jewish families is described in these affecting lines, pregnant with dumb sorrow :

> O daughter of Israel, who knows thy life? In darkness thou comest, and in darkness goest. Thy sufferings, thy joy, thy pain, thy hopes are born and die within thyself. All the choicest gifts of earth, all happiness and ease are lavished on the daughters of other nations; but the life of the Jewess is everlasting slavery; she goes not a step outside her shop. Conceive, bear, suckle, wean, cook and bake—and wither all too soon: that is her lot.

What has the Jewish woman to do with love? All a woman needs is to know how to cook and bear children. For her any kind of education is superfluous, or even positively sinful. She is not consulted about what most affects her whole future : Bath-Shua is not asked whether she wishes to marry Hillel or not. Like a true Jewish wife, Bath-Shua is faithful to her unloved husband, whose only study is the Talmud. The family grows in number, and its means of support grow less; and Hillel at last decides to go and seek his fortune in foreign parts. For some time after leaving he writes " love-letters " to his wife; then he stops writing altogether, and all trace of him is lost. Bath-Shua, still young and beautiful, remains an *Agunah*, that is, a woman bound for life to a husband who has disappeared, and with no right to marry again.

Salvation appears in the shape of the engineer Fabi, who falls in love with Bath-Shua. When he learns of her misfortune, he makes enquiries until he succeeds in discovering the place where this husband lives who has deserted her and her children. For five hundred roubles Hillel agrees to give Bath-Shua a writ of divorce. After the writ has been received, news comes that Hillel has gone down in a ship sunk at sea. Bath-Shua is already betrothed to Fabi, and they are greatly attached to one another. But the course of true love does not run smoothly: Rabbi Vofsi sees to that. He has examined the writ and found that it is improperly drafted: according to the *Shulhan Arukh* the name Hillel should be written with a *yod*, even though this offends against the elementary laws of grammar. This dubious *yod* is absent in the writ, therefore Bath-Shua is still the wife of Hillel. Since Hillel has been lost at sea, the law does not allow his death to be presumed. Thus the happiness of Bath-Shua and her children and the happiness of Fabi are shattered by the dubious *yod* of inhumanly rigorous legalism.

There could be no more scathing and contemptuous indictment of the blunted sensibilities of the rabbis, no more luminous and convincing demonstration of the pressing need for reform in the Jewish religion, than is to be found in this great poem.

Gordon did not make war only on the rabbis and the *Shulhan Arukh*. In his *Two Josephs ben Simeon* he castigates not the rabbis but the Jewish community leaders; and in his *Shomereth Yabam* he exposes the evils wrought by the domination of the self-seeking rabbis appointed by the Russian Government. Gordon desired reforms not in religious matters only, but also in the spheres of education and Jewish communal affairs. To secure such reforms he relied on one well-tried and irresistible weapon—a keen, penetrating satire, sometimes resembling that of Voltaire, and sometimes that of Heine. He was a satirist of great power, without an equal among Hebrew poets.

In these latter articles and poems Gordon entirely abandoned the Biblical style, which, with all its beauty and poetry, is not adapted to descriptions of modern life. His later style draws largely on the inexhaustible wealth of the truly popular idiom to be found in the Talmud and related literature, an idiom somewhat reminiscent of the German-Jewish jargon. Quips, witticisms and puns pour freely from his pen, to confound the orthodox and dispel the prevailing darkness.

While Gordon the satirist has been excelled by none except Abramowitz, Gordon the humorist has a strong rival in Mordecai

David BRANDSTAEDTER (1844-1928), one of the chief contributors to *Ha-Shahar*. Many of Brandstaedter's short stories rank very high in Hebrew literature, and have deservedly been chosen for translation into Russian and English (*Mordecai Kizowitch, The Jew-Hater of Gryleff, Dr. Joseph Alfasi*, etc.). He does not penetrate deeply into the hearts of his characters, and he knows more of their outer doings than of the spirit and inwardness of their lives. On the other hand, he can describe with lively humour every movement and every expression of the Hasidim of Galicia, their crude superstitions and prejudices, their appalling fanaticism, the wiliness of their cunning wonder-working saints, the *Zaddiks*, and the malpractices and unscrupulous dealings of their community leaders. Besides the Hasidim and ultra-orthodox, he presents on his stage the sham aristocracy, the ignorant upstarts, who have acquired only the veneer of western culture, and nothing of its reality; and against these, too, he is unsparing in his satire. Some of his stories touch on more moving and serious topics, like *Dr. Alfasi* or *Sidonia*; yet even there glimpses of a healthy, hearty humour emerge. Until the 'eighties, Brandstaedter was really the only humorist in Hebrew literature: Erter, Abramowitz and Gordon were satirists rather than humorists.

Judah Löb LEWIN (1845-1926), a poet already mentioned, was a frequent contributor to *Ha-Shahar*. In his poems, *Elhanan* and *Practical Ability*, which have a socialist flavour, the influence of Nekrasow is apparent, as it is also in certain of Gordon's poems. Dr. Solomon MANDELKERN (1855-1902) also published several interesting ballads in *Ha-Shahar*, one of which, *Come, my love*! is somewhat reminiscent of Goethe's *Erlkönig* (which the younger Lebensohn had translated under the title *The King of Terrors*). An orphan boy went to the synagogue one Friday evening with his uncle, and fell asleep during the prayers. His uncle forgot about him and went home alone. After some time had elapsed the uncle remembered the orphan and had search made for him; and when they had looked everywhere else in vain they went to search for him in the synagogue, which had been shut up for some time, and there found him lying dead. The child had been frightened to death by the dark shadows of terror with which cabbalistic superstition had peopled the very synagogue.

Others who played an important part in the pages of *Ha-Shahar* were Eleazar SCHULMAN (1837-1903), a versatile writer and the author of biographies—*From the Stock of Israel*—of Heine (1876) and Börne (1894), of a host of articles packed with learning, and of stories that were not so successful; Judah Löb KANTOR (1849-1917), later famous as the producer of the first Hebrew daily newspaper, *Ha-Yom*, in which, as also in *Ha-*

Shiloah, he wrote miscellaneous articles, notable for their amusing subject-matter and attractive style; and Mordecai Ben Hillel HAKOHEN, later known as one of the best of the *Hibbat-Zion* school of writers. Among other publicists and critics of merit were Yehiel BERNSTEIN and Pesach RUDERMANN. Noteworthy among the scholars who collaborated in *Ha-Shahar* was David KAHANA (1838-1915), who, besides various articles on the Bible, published in *Ha-Shahar* his famous " Stones " series—*The Stone of the Wanderers, The Stone of Stumbling, The Stone of Darkness*—treating of the pseudo-messiah Shabbethai Zevi and of Cabbalah and Hasidism in the 16th, 17th and 18th Centuries (later collected together in a single volume entitled " History of the Cabbalists, Shabbethæans and Hasidim," Odessa 1913-14, 3rd ed. Tel-Aviv, 1926). Another regular contributor to *Ha-Shahar* was the Galician scholar Solomon RUBIN (1823-1910), who spent a long lifetime on the history of the religions and superstitions of all races, ancient and modern, and dissipated the mystical sanctity of religious superstitions and prejudices by revealing their historical origin and growth.

Even more valuable from this point of view were the scholarly researches of Isaac Hirsch WEISS (1815-1905), author of the five-volume work *Dor Dor v'Dor'shav* (" The Generations and their Expounders," 1871-1891; reprinted

1924). In this monumental work Weiss examined exhaustively the continuous evolution of the Oral Law, from the origin of the Jewish nation to its expulsion from Spain, thus presenting an account of the religious achievement of the Jewish genius throughout the ages. Reuben Brainin has well said that Weiss did for " the Science of Judaism " what Darwin did for natural science. Here for the first time the course of evolutionary development in Judaism was correctly traced. The book created a profound impression on contemporary readers. The uncritical students of the rabbinical seminaries, brought up on the Talmud and its commentators, thought that the Talmud had sprung into being as a complete whole; they did not recognise in it any stratification, any chronological sequence, any gradual change under the influence of varying conditions. Weiss's research showed them the Talmud as a product of the human mind and the national life, worthy, indeed, of the highest admiration, but liable to change and modification at different times and in different countries. Thus a new light was shed on the whole of Jewish religious literature.

A similar light had been shed on the Talmud somewhat earlier by Zachariah FRANKEL (1801-1875) in his Hebrew books, *Dar'khé ha-Mishnah* (1859) and *Mebo ha-Yerushalmi* (1870), and in many works written in German. This great scholar not only traced the historical relation of the Mishnah to the scriptures, but also described the individual characteristics of each of the *Tannaim*, the teachers who created the whole of the Oral Law. Thus the foundation of all the extensive researches in the earliest Jewish literature was laid in the revived Hebrew language.

CHAPTER IV

THE PERIOD OF NATIONALISM

The dominant note of the literature of militant *Haskalah* was one of negation rather than of affirmation: therein lay its most serious defect. To break down the " Chinese wall " and to destroy antiquated prejudices was no doubt at the time a necessary and valuable piece of work; it was in reality a great positive achievement. But many of the writers of the 'sixties and 'seventies adopted a hostile or contemptuous attitude towards anything typically and specifically Jewish, began to seek their ideals exclusively outside Jewish life and Judaism, and developed an exaggerated respect for all that was non-Jewish. In their zeal for Europeanisation they made no distinction between those elements of European civilisation to which the Jews, as human beings and a living race, were really bound to adapt themselves, and those external forms and habits which threatened to undermine the distinctive Jewish type of social and national life. The younger generation, apt pupils of their favourite authors, broke away in large numbers, and almost became bitter enemies of their own people. Both the authors themselves and their young followers failed to understand the value of Judaism as a historically developed culture and civilisation, and to realise that the unique life of the Jewish race in the past marked out the line of its future development. A nation that had played its part in all the great movements of humanity throughout two thousand years could not segregate itself from the general cultural progress of mankind; but, on the other hand, a nation that had always gone its own peculiar way, and had made important contributions to human culture, must fuse European civilisation and its own specifically national culture into an organic whole. This last point was not understood by most of the Jewish writers of the 'sixties and 'seventies, with the result that the ideal of assimilation to European culture was their only positive contribution to the solution of their people's problems. Hence the younger generation failed to find positive ideals in Jewish life, and began to look for them outside. The consequence was that many young Jews threw themselves into revolutionary movements which had no direct connection with their own people, or became absorbed in medicine, law, literature or science, and were lost. Judaism was deserted either for non-Jewish ideals, or for the more vulgar ambitions of the career-hunter. For most of the *Maskilim*, *Haskalah* became merely a key to personal advancement, an art and a business in itself. The writers who had fought the battle of *Haskalah* had aimed at giving their people intellectual freedom; with bitter regret they saw the new generation of *Maskilim* develop into materialists and self-seekers, caring for nothing but success and wealth. Lilienblum and Gordon had demanded that certain religious customs should be abolished in conformity with the changed outlook of the younger generation; but actually the younger generation had entirely cast away religion and was given over to frivolity and self-indulgence. Judaism, and with it the Hebrew language and literature, had fallen on evil days; and if this state of things continued unchanged, the new Hebrew literature of the period of the *Haskalah* controversy was bound to become extinct. So it is not surprising that there soon came a reaction against most of the ideals of the iconoclastic *Maskilim*.

Such a reaction began in the early 'seventies. From the time of M. A. Günzburg we find the Russian Jews imitating their brethren in Germany, among whom external and internal causes had combined to give a great impetus to the Reform movement before any demand for religious reforms was put forward by the Russian and Galician Hebrew writers. The general tendency of these writers was to look upon the western Jews as an exalted and almost unapproachable model. The Hebrew advocates of *Haskalah* cast admiring and envious eyes on the Europeanised community organisations of the western Jews, their fine modern " Temples," their cultured and scholarly rabbis and preachers, and so forth.

But in 1868 Peretz SMOLENSKIN (1842-1885), then twenty-six years old, came to Vienna, after visiting Berlin, Paris and London, and was able to look at " enlightened " Judaism for himself, and to study at close quarters the life of the " reformed " Jews. He found, to his astonishment, that this Judaism was nothing but an empty and meaningless show, influencing neither heart nor brain. He found that the "enlightened " Jews had snapped the bond that united them with the rest of their brethren, that they had abandoned the national language and given up the great national hope—the idea of national redemption. He heard that they had invented a sophistical theory that they were " Germans of the Jewish religion," and yet, at the same time, did not wish to observe, or even properly to understand, this " Jewish religion." What connection, then, had they with Judaism? Was it only an empty name? Or were they, perhaps, tied to the Jewish " religion " by some deeper instinct, which no sophistry could overcome or set at naught, by an unconscious national instinct?

He saw the Reform Synagogues—and found them empty. The warm, spontaneous religious feeling of the simple Jew had vanished. Its place was taken by the Rabbi-

Preacher, who expounded from his pulpit the policy of Bismarck; by the "Cantor," who was merely an opera-singer, the Christian choir-girls, who accompanied the prayers, part Hebrew and part German, and the organ, played by a gentile; these were the " reforms," and they had converted the synagogue into a concert-hall. It was all artificial, all false, all imitation. There was nothing in it that was truly of the people, nothing that sprang from the living Jewish heart. Yet the Western Jewish scholars went on repeating their well-worn phrase, that the Jews were " a light to the Gentiles," because they had given humanity monotheism and a lofty ethic, while all the time they were given over, heart and soul, to an alien culture, a foreign morality, and an alien mode of life. And Smolenskin asked himself, Can a great people live on its past alone, with no hope of a bright future? Can it consider itself not a nation, but only a religious group?

In 1869 Smolenskin founded the monthly periodical *Ha-Shahar* ("The Dawn "), which died only (1884) with its editor's last breath. In his very first article, in which he lays down the paper's programme, we hear a note quite different from that struck by his contemporaries. He writes, in his semi-poetical style: " Just as I have stretched out my hand against the hypocritical and sanctimonious, who garb themselves in holiness and yet try to make understanding cease from the House of Jacob, so, too, do I raise my hand against the hypocritical and sophisticated, who with their smooth tongues entice the children of Israel away from the inheritance of their fathers." Later he goes on to say, " Lo, they tell us, Let us be like all other nations! I, too, repeat it after them : Let us be like all other nations in pursuing and acquiring knowledge, in forsaking the way of wickedness and folly, in being faithful citizens in the lands where we are scattered, but let us also be like all other nations in not being ashamed of the quarry whence we were hewn; let us be like all other nations in treasuring our language and our nation's honour! There is no shame and no reproach in our belief that some day an end will be made of our exile, that some day the kingdom shall return to the house of Israel, just as no other nation is ashamed to live in expectation of freeing itself from the hands of strangers .... We feel no shame in holding tight to the ancient language that has gone about with us from nation to nation, and in which our seers and poets have sung. . . ."

Thus was the positive programme of nationalism enunciated for the first time in Hebrew literature with the rise of " The Dawn."

Smolenskin soon began to publish in *Ha-Shahar* a long series of articles and books, such as *The Stone of Israel, The Eternal*

People and *Time to Plant*, which constitute the beginning of a new era in Hebrew literature, the era of nationalism. His *Eternal People* (1872) is specially important. It is the basis of the Hebrew national movement. Smolenskin's conception of nationalism is not narrow or chauvinistic. For him nationalism is the antithesis of cosmopolitanism—the notion that all mankind is one large conglomeration of human beings, in which specific group-characteristics and the differentiations due to climate and historical causes can be ignored; but it is in no way opposed to universalism— the idea of human equality and brotherhood. Family love, for example, is quite compatible with love of mankind. Nationality is a progressive and not a reactionary force. The greater the number of forms and varieties and the greater the diversification, the greater the advance. The degree of development and the human value of the individual increase as he becomes more complex and self-dependent. Then why should we aim at the elimination of individual groups with distinct characteristics in humanity at large? The various nations are such individual groups, and the sum of their distinctive qualities, and the continuous influence of each of them on the others, are what constitute the civilisation of the human species.

The Jews also are a nation. This Smolenskin proves clearly and conclusively in his *Time to Plant*. Here he attacks the theory of Moses Mendelssohn and his followers, who held that the Jews were only a religious body, or, at the most, that their primary concern was religion, and not nationalism and its cultural expressions. Smolenskin does not, indeed, deny that it was by its peculiar religion that the Jewish people lived through its two thousand years of wandering; but for him this religion is not the antithesis of nationalism, but is itself a part of Jewish nationalism. And as nationalism is always conditioned by time and place, so the Jewish national religion has developed in the course of history and adapted itself to different ages and environments. Thus the Jewish religion is to be regarded as a collection of religious and moral concepts, which are but the quintessence of the creations of the Hebrew national spirit. The Jewish religion is not a moral philosophy understandable only by a few choice spirits; nor is it a set of lifeless dogmas, the monopoly of a priesthood. It is the *Welt-Anschauung* of a nation, something intimate and comprehensible to all. Hence Smolenskin opposes, on the one side, the " credalists " like Maimonides and Moses Mendelssohn, who did not admit the gradual historical development of Judaism, and, on the other, the Reformers, who disregarded this gradual development. He, too, demands reforms, but internal reforms only, based on the marked changes which had recently taken place in the national life and on the popular demands which were the outcome of these changes. There is no value in religious reforms required only by the more "enlightened" and the " aristocracy," who, after all, do not observe even the few rules left untouched by the Reformers. When Luther effected reforms in Roman Catholic Christianity he was himself a believer, as were also the masses of the people; but the reform-rabbis and the advocates of *Haskalah* had long since lost all spontaneous religious feeling, while the Jewish populace, which still retained this feeling, had no wish at all for external reforms. So Smolenskin cries: Teach your children our national tongue, try to implant in them the spirit of our religion, or rather, the spirit of our culture, of which religion is but a part, although an important part—then the coming generation will cease of its own accord to venerate the dead letter of the law and to observe its dry rules; then, with the national spirit strong and alive in your children, they will not cease to be Jews even when they have ceased to be orthodox.

Such is the fundamental idea of *The Eternal People*, Smolenskin's most important propagandist book. His *Time to Plant* is only a supplement to it, and is spoilt, like most of his books and articles, by its prolixity, by having been written piecemeal and hastily at odd moments, and by lack of revision, so that there is a great deal of repetition of the same thing in different words.

Smolenskin knew that a people could not

live on its ancient culture alone; it must have ideals that belong to the present and a national hope of a better future. The Jewish nation had, indeed, such ideals and hopes, though they had been forgotten or half-effaced by lapse of time. The most eloquent section in *The Eternal People* is that on "The Hope of Israel." Here he describes the nature of the Messianic idea which had kept up the spirit of the Jewish people in its darkest days. During the Exile the hope of national redemption had become too unreal, too mystical and intangible; but it could be purged of the rank growth of cabbalist ideas, and then it would again illumine the path of the Jews in their wanderings. As in his outline of the policy of *Ha-Shahar*, so also in *The Eternal People*, Smolenskin speaks of the possibility of national revival in Palestine. History knows no impossibilities; this has been shown by the revival of the Greeks, and of the uncultured Serbs and Montenegrins. All that the Jews lack is a feeling of unity among all sections of the people. Once this feeling is aroused, everything will become possible. We thus find the germ of Zionism as a nationalist idea in Smolenskin many years before it emerged as a national movement.

In this Smolenskin was not alone. In 1871, a year before *The Eternal People* was published, David GORDON (1826-1886), assistant editor of *Ha-Maggid*, the first Hebrew periodical, wrote a series of articles on the settlement of Jews in Palestine as a basis of the future revival of the whole Jewish people. About the same time as *The Eternal People* there appeared a pamphlet by Yehiel Michal PINES (1845-1913) entitled *Sons of my Spirit* (Mayence, 1872), in which the writer attacks the negative attitude adopted by Hebrew authors towards the Jewish religion. For Pines Jewish observance is full of profound poetry, of healthy and ingrown popular feeling; and he argues that it is thanks to this poetical element alone that the Jews have been able to endure their hell of sufferings and to survive as a cultured race. Pines apparently realised that the religious customs in themselves had no national value, but he was convinced that they ought to be observed so that the underlying abstract ideas might find practical embodiment; then and only then could these ideas take form as the Jewish people's way of life. The relation between religious ideas and practical ceremonial is that between the flame and the wick. The wick at first sight may seem of no importance at all, since in itself it is merely so much crude material; but without it flame is impossible. This, we have seen, was also S. D. Luzzatto's idea; but Pines was a far more orthodox Jew than Luzzatto. Like other romantic reactionaries, he wanted to justify the religious position in its entirety, and urged the observance of *all* the ceremonial laws, since in all of them he could perceive a poetical content. The nationalism of Pines was a conservative nationalism; Smolenskin's was progressive. Smolenskin was no reactionary, though he parted company with the militant protagonists of *Haskalah* and their shallow philosophy. He, no less than they, hurls his criticism at the hypocritical rabbis of all kinds, and the various communal leaders and officials. None could describe the degraded spiritual conditions and the ugliness of the *Heders* and *Yeshivahs* as he could; but, at the same time, he was aware of the light that still shone in Judaism and that was preserved especially in the *Yeshivah*.

Smolenskin wrote six long novels and several short stories. The novels have serious defects. The plot is always complicated and unnatural; there are numerous hiatuses; the characters are not so much living human beings or psychological types, as mouthpieces of the author. Their individuality is completely submerged under the weight of the writer's social purpose. Yet Smolenskin's novels have much value. They mirror faithfully the condition of the various strata of society in a small Lithuanian township in the 'sixties. And individual descriptions, as, for example, of the *Yeshivahs*, are remarkable for their truth and realism.

His best known novel is *The Wanderer through the Paths of Life*, a story in four volumes. Its hero, "the wanderer," is an orphan, whom fortune has made dependent on the kindness of various " kind people." He is thrown into various spheres of society, but nowhere does he find anybody who can show him which is the right way of life to choose. The reader is shown a terrible picture of contemporary Jewish life, in which the remote villages of Lithuania are portrayed with all their sordidness, with all their meanness and degradation, with all the pettiness of their so-called spiritual leaders.

The orphan first falls into the hands of a cunning and fraudulent wonder-worker, and the boy soon sees through his unscrupulous trickery, masked though it is under the guise of sanctity. He joins a company of wandering beggars, and their life, terrible in its moral emptiness, though free and full of unexpected adventures and greedy, high-spirited jollity, is depicted in close and faithful detail, and sometimes with inimitable humour. He then hires himself as a chorister to a synagogue precentor, and again he encounters the grotesque and debased life of the Ghetto. Later we find him grown up into a *Bahur*, a student in the *Yeshivah*—the Jewish academy or university; and the life of the *Yeshivah* students, the " great lights " destined to be rabbis and spiritual powers in Israel, is shown us with all its shortcomings, the inevitable result, on the one hand, of ceaseless study in a single dry subject, without any change or relief, and, on the other, of the unhealthy economic position of the *Yeshivah* student, who lives on the bounty of private persons under the system known by the curious Yiddish name *essen Täg*, " eating days," i.e. free board, in which he eats his meals at a different house each day of the week. All the arrangements, or rather disarrangements, of the *Yeshivah* are vividly described by Smolenskin, who, however, sees the good side as well as the bad. " The wanderer " also suffers all the terrors of the " cantonist " period, when Jewish children were carried off into military service, in the time of the Czar Nicholas I, " a time wherein one man had power over another to his hurt " (Eccles., 8, 9). Of this flagrant violation of the Jew's human rights Smolenskin speaks with a prophet's indignation, almost choking with suppressed anger and tears.

In his early manhood " the wanderer " is thrown together with a depraved Hasid, and after a long series of episodes and mishaps he comes to London, where he gets to know the "enlightened" Jews of free England. He finds that they are indeed free of prejudices and narrow orthodoxy, but that at the same time they have lost their authentic Jewishness.

Thus there is no sphere of Jewish life, high or low, which is not described in *The Wanderer*. It was not without reason that when the first three parts appeared (1871; the fourth part was added in 1876) they provoked so much discussion, and that a large number of periodicals in different languages warmly welcomed the book and saw in it, despite its defects, the beginning of a new era in Hebrew literature. The younger generation read it with avidity, and made much of its tiniest detail. Many parts of it were learnt by heart. The orthodox, on the other hand, burnt it, and looked upon Smolenskin as the worst kind of " epicurean." *The Wanderer*, indeed, had no pity on orthodoxy and criticised it mercilessly. But Smolenskin already stood at the parting of the ways. On the one hand, as a progressive writer and a child of his time, he fought vigorously against the old manner of life, based as it was on the dead letter and on antiquated ceremonial laws; but, on the other hand, it is enough to read the chapter in *The Wanderer* dealing with Yom Kippur, the Day of Atonement, to be convinced that he too, like Luzzatto and Pines, appreciated to the full the worth and beauty of the magic poetry enshrined in the finest manifestations of Jewish religious emotion. For this reason Smolenskin became the idol of the younger generation : he was nothing less than the founder of that progressive nationalist tendency in Hebrew literature which takes from traditional Judaism only what is fine and noble, and for which nationalism is not a reactionary reversion to an antiquated past, nor a movement towards separation from other peoples, but a forward movement, a vital aspiration to bring to life and fulness those aspects of Judaism as a universal historic force which are of absolute human value.

Artistically Smolenskin's second novel, *The Burial of an Ass* (1874), is a great advance on *The Wanderer*. Its plot is not so elaborately constructed, yet as a story it is more interesting. The fundamental problem with which it deals—the conflict between the individual and the community—raises it above the ordinary, and its artistic treatment of this interesting theme entitles it to rank as a classic. Much inferior, artistically, is his *Reward of the Righteous* (1876), treating of the Polish rebellion against Russia and the share in the rebellion of " the Poles of Jewish faith." The empty promises of the real Poles, who were ungrateful to their faithful allies, the Jews, leads the reader to the conclusion that no trust can be put in " the kindness of the gentiles." The novel is a kind of preliminary to the idea of self-deliverance from the *Galuth*, and from this point of view it is interesting and important: it is the truest expression of the state of feeling in this transition period. The last and greatest of Smolenskin's novels, *The Inheritance* (1878-1884), which he finished on his death-bed, closes on the Zionist note. But it is in his story *The Vengeance of the Covenant* (1884) that Smolenskin best depicts the transition of the younger generation from the ideal of assimilation to that of Zionism. Here he describes the pogroms of 1881-82, sets forth those nationalist ideas which had captured the younger Jews even before the pogroms took place, and appraises the influence of these outbreaks in bringing back the Jewish " intelligentsia " to Judaism and in promoting the revival of old ideals in a new form.

In 1879, two years before the pogroms, two articles appeared in *Ha-Shahar* by a young student in Paris, afterwards to become so famous—Eliezer BEN YEHUDA (1858-1922). The writer's thesis was that the settlement of Jews in Palestine was the best means of securing national and political centralisation of all the scattered people of Israel, the one and only anchor of safety for Jews and Judaism alike. These articles were no doubt prompted by the events of 1878 (the Russian war with Turkey for the freedom of the Balkan peoples), and also, perhaps, by George Eliot's Zionist novel, *Daniel Deronda* (1876).

Thus, by the end of the 'seventies, all was in readiness, from the point of view of development within Hebrew literature, for the complete revolution that ushered in a new period.

CHAPTER V
THE PERIOD OF REVIVAL

With the 'eighties Hebrew literature enters on a new period of development. Till then it had been little more than a means of propagating *Haskalah* among the Jews. Although it embraced every possible form of literary composition it was not an end in itself; that is to say, it was not a national literature in the wider sense, taking the whole of the people's life for its province, and including the whole range of cultural self-expression that sprang from the roots of the national being. It was simply a means of improving the condition of those individual Jews who understood no other language. Hence, after *Haskalah* had become widespread among the Jews of Russia and Galicia, and the newly educated class among them began to understand Russian or German, it seemed as though Hebrew literature had ceased to be needed and had lost its value, and might be put on the shelf in Russia and Galicia, as it had already been in Germany.

But early in the 'eighties the emergence of the *Hibbath Zion* ("Love of Zion") idea saved Hebrew literature from such a sorry fate. *Hibbath Zion* laid down three principles. In the first place, the Jews are a single people in spite of their being dispersed to the four corners of the earth; and even those Jews who have no reasoned conviction of the unity of the Jewish people still feel it in their hearts —or are given tangible proof of its existence by the anti-Semites. Secondly, since the Jews have never found a resting place in the countries of their dispersion, they must create a national and political centre which, by virtue of being established in the historic home of the Jewsh race, will be equally precious to all Jews throughout the world. Thirdly, in this historical national centre, where the Hebrew language had left an ineffaceable impress, the united people must revive its ancient tongue, so that it may continue its creative activity in its historical language, and may be saved from the confusion of tongues which must otherwise result when Jews, speaking the various languages of the five continents, foregather in this national centre. Hence it is in this national language, and no other, that the literature of the Jews, both " Jewish " and " general," must be written. Thereby Hebrew literature will become one long chain, having as its first link the Hebrew Bible, and its last link shrouded in the mists of the future. The four thousand years of Jewish history demand as their correlative a literature of forty centuries.

Thus the revival of the Hebrew language and literature was an essential factor in the *Hibbath Zion* movement, which, without it, would be utterly inconceivable.

Ben Yehuda, who had begun to preach *Hibbath Zion* even before the pogroms, was the first to revive Hebrew as a spoken language, to modernise it and widen the scope of Hebrew literature. He began this revival of spoken Hebrew himself, in his own home. One morning he began to speak only Hebrew to his wife, who knew not a word of the national language. She rubbed her eyes, and after grasping with some difficulty what his purpose was, she explained to him, in Russian, that she too would gladly learn to speak Hebrew, only she could not suddenly make herself dumb: a new language must be introduced gradually. But he was adamant. A year later Hebrew speech began to echo within the walls of Ben Yehuda's house. Still more, Ben Yehuda and his wife Deborah pledged themselves to speak only in Hebrew with all their acquaintances who understood the language. A few years later Deborah Ben Yehuda became a Hebrew teacher in one of the Jerusalem schools. Many of the *Maskilim* in Jerusalem, Jaffa and some of the Jewish colonies in Palestine imitated Ben Yehuda's example. Practical necessity reinforced the idealism of the revivalists. Side by side lived Russians, Poles, Galicians and Hungarians, who spoke the German-Jewish jargon; Sephardi Jews, who spoke the Spanish-Hebrew jargon (Spaniolish); Jews from the Yemen and Morocco, who spoke Arabic; Caucasian Jews who spoke a Tartar dialect; also Jews

HEBREW LITERATURE

who spoke Persian and even Aramaic. How could Jews speaking such diverse tongues understand one another unless there was a common language acceptable to all alike? This need for a common " inter-territorial " language was felt especially in the Palestinian schools, to which these Jews of diverse languages sent their children. Through this combination of idealism and practical necessity Hebrew became the language of instruction in all the newer Jewish schools of Palestine; and from the schools the language passed into daily life. This happened not only in Palestine; from the 'nineties onwards Hebrew was increasingly spoken in the Diaspora, and in recent years Hebrew-speaking has spread with great rapidity.

The resuscitation of spoken Hebrew involved the need of new words and expressions to denote objects unknown in ancient times, and to express clearly and exactly all the new ideas and all the nuances and fine shades of modern thought and feeling. In writing it was always possible to evade the difficulty arising from inadequate vocabulary by means of periphrasis or allusion. Thus in written Hebrew it was possible to tolerate and become accustomed to a euphuistic and archaic phraseology (*Melitzah*). This was the manner of Erter and Mapu, who dressed up their modern descriptions and ideas in the ancient poetical style of the Bible; and the same thing was done to some extent by Gordon and Lilienblum, who made use of the language of the Talmud and related literatures. But it was impossible for Ben Yehuda, who habitually spoke Hebrew and published a newspaper covering the widest range of topics (*Ha-Zevi;* later *Ha-Or* and *Hashkaphah*), to rest content with an imitation of a language of ancient times.

Thus the task of widening the scope of the language devolved on Ben Yehuda. He introduced very many new words into the old, yet still young, language, as the Ibn-Tibbon family of translators had done in the 12th and 13th centuries. A special section in his newspaper was devoted to the extension and enrichment of the language by means of Hebrew words to be found in the Talmudic and mediæval literature, by means of Arabic words of pure Semitic pedigree, and finally, by invented words fashioned according to the canons of the language which prevailed at the time when it had not wholly ceased to be spoken.

The problem of extending and modernising the language became a matter of sharp controversy between the old and the new schools. The older Hebrew writers, purists, upholders of " Hebrew undefiled," for whom, far though they often were from orthodoxy, Hebrew was still "the holy language," would not permit themselves any neologisms; the younger writers, the " modernisers," who had no regard for the " sanctity " of the national language, did their best to extend it and adapt it to modern requirements and European modes of thought. For the Jewish people, returning to a new life in its ancestral land, exactly as in the case of modern Greece and emancipated Norway, the problem of extending and modernising the language became a national problem and a crucial test of progress or retrogression from the religious and nationalist point of view.

The Hebrew literature of the 'eighties stood out as the antithesis of the literature of the *Haskalah* period. Thanks to pogroms in Russia and anti-Semitism in Western Europe, which made no distinction between the orthodox and the enlightened and free-thinking Jew, many of the *Maskilim* began to scrutinise the hitherto accepted tenets of *Haskalah*. Inevitably they reached the conclusion that *Haskalah* and Europeanisation were not synonymous with high standards of character; they also recognised more and more clearly that high standards of moral character had always been the characteristic possession of genuine Judaism. Crude attacks on Judaism by the " enlightened " and " learned " European Jewish writers stirred up a goodly number of the younger *Maskilim* in defence of their people's honour and aroused their national pride. They began to remember that it was this persecuted and vilified Judaism that had given humanity the Prophets, Hillel and Spinoza. A return to Judaism together with a return to Palestine, the historic fatherland of Judaism—such was the aspiration of these younger nationalist Jews. Some of them formed the first group of pioneers to go and settle in Palestine, a group known as the " Bilu " (a word made up of the initials of the words *Beth Ya'akob l'khu v'nel'kha*, Isaiah 2, 5—"O house of Jacob, come and let us walk [in the light of the Lord]". They made their goal the revival of the Land by the nation, and the revival of the nation by the Land—by means of honest toil, work on the land, and contact with mother earth, with creative and healing nature, from which the Jews had been torn by exile, persecution and oppressive laws. They aimed also at reviving what was good in ancient Judaism, at giving their nation its positive values, the " light " that shone in it, the light that the negative writers of the *Haskalah* period had failed to recognise. This was the good and progressive side of *Hibbath Zion*, the effect of which was apparent in the Hebrew literature of the 'eighties, the epoch of revival.

But the early members of the *Hibbath Zion* movement, in their love for historic Judaism and their opposition to the tenets of the *Maskilim* of the 'sixties and 'seventies, went from one extreme to the other. If the *Maskilim* were too iconoclastic, the " Lovers of Zion " were too conservative : they developed an affection for many things which, although history had set the seal of sanctity on them, were not truly deserving of affection at all. In the literature of the 'eighties a reactionary current set in, sweeping along with it many of the best of those who had fought in the cause of *Haskalah*. Gordon alone remained true to his ideas till the end of his life. *Hibbath Zion*, which exercised a decisive influence on the new literature, was thus marked by two tendencies, differing from each other yet springing from a single source. On one side was the general reversion to the past, complete and unchanged—reaction and retrogression; on the other side was " revival," a longing for what was good in the past, in the age of the Prophets, with which there might be combined whatever was good and noble in the present, that is to say, whatever was good and worthy in modern European civilisation. These two tendencies stood in opposition to each other throughout the 'eighties and the 'nineties, and the struggle between them is not yet over.

In 1882 Gordon completed twenty-five years of literary work, and the occasion was elaborately celebrated by the *Maskilim* of St. Petersburg (Leningrad), who previously had seemed to have long since severed all connection with Hebrew literature. A new spirit came over the famous poet: he felt that the day of the nation's revival and unity was near at hand, and he wrote the enthusiastic poem *Young and old we will go.*

We were one people, one people will we be!
We are all hewn from the same quarry; we have
shared joy and sorrow these two thousand years,
since we were scattered. And from nation to
nation, from province to province, young and old
we will go!

Each man goes his own way on the paths of
life, seeking his pasture where he finds it; he
wrongs his friend, and tramples on his brother,
for each is dearer to himself than his neighbour.
But when the voice of our God calls us, we will
go, young and old!

One people are we, for we have one God, and
are hewn of the same quarry; one Torah and one
language we have, and by these golden chains are
we linked. So, bound by this three-fold cord,
we will go, young and old!

Old and young, wise and simple, rich and poor,
we will rally to our holy banner, like the poor
sheep when the storm breaks. The storm makes
no distinction of prince and pauper—young and
old we will go!

The storm breaks, the gale roars, the tumultuous waters all but engulf us. Have no fear,
Jacob, nor let thy soul be downcast! Myriads of
men will not submit to slaughter! Out of the
storm calls the voice of our God—we will go,
young and old!

Hold we fast to our God, forsake we not His
faith, nor let our lips forget His holy tongue!
We have seen evil and shall yet see good, we shall
yet live again in the Land as once we lived. If
God has decreed that we take hold of the
wanderer's staff again, young and old we will go!

At that time the entire Jewish world was
inspired by the hope of a new national

unity, and of the rehabilitation of the historic language, to which this poem gives expression. In 1886 there appeared the first daily Hebrew paper, *Ha-Yom*, founded by Judah Löb Kantor. Through its editor's leaders and David FRISCHMANN's feuilletons it introduced a new, European tone into Hebrew literature. Soon afterwards the two papers *Ha-Melitz* and *Ha-Tzefirah* began to appear daily on the lines of the great European newspapers. *Ha-Tzefirah* came almost entirely under the control of Nahum SOKOLOW (b. 1859), the first European journalist in the Hebrew world, who wielded his gifted pen first as political editor, later as leader-writer and feuilletonist. His essays and causeries were remarkable for their rich and colourful style. SOKOLOW also edited the literary annual *Ha-Asif* (1884-1894), which dealt with a wide range of topics and exerted much influence. A similar collection, devoted to *Hibbath Zion*, was *K'nesseth Israel* (1886-1888), produced by the translator of Graetz's *History of the Jews*, Saul Phineas RABINOWITZ (1844-1910); while the annual, *Otzar ha-Sifruth* (1887-1896), published in Galicia by Eisig GRAEBER, was chiefly devoted to the "Science of Judaism."

In Hebrew poetry too the new note was soon heard. In 1885 appeared a striking ballad by Constantine Asher SHAPIRA (1841-1900), *Visions of the Daughter of my People*. Just as the Germans cherish a legend that their heroic king, the idol of the popular imagination, Friedrich Barbarossa, never died, but sleeps in Kyffhäuser, so the Jews cannot believe that the victorious king, "the sweet singer of Israel," could die like other men. No, king David is still alive! He is not dead, but only bound with golden fetters, awaiting the hour when redemption shall come; then he will rouse himself, break the golden fetters and appear before his people as the king-Messiah for whose coming the outcasts of Israel have longed in the countries of their exile. Shapira treats this wonderful legend with much skill. His ballad breathes the spirit of the time—a longing for national redemption, an ardent love of the popular legends and of the uncontaminated Hebrew tradition which the champions of *Haskalah* had treated so cavalierly. Shapira also published a series of poems under the general title *Songs of Jeshurun*, which are distinguished by their lyric feeling, delicate style and dignified pathos.

Two other Hebrew poets came on the scene at the same time. One of them was the leading poet of the *Hibbath Zion* movement, whose muse was so tuned that he sang only of Jewish sorrows and sufferings and the hope of redemption, and never of any other human interest. This was Menahem Dolitzky (1856-1931), whose *On the Hills of Zion*, *I have desired of Thee*, and *If I forget Thee*, have become almost folk-songs. Dolitzky knows nothing of love or nature, or of the personal human feelings which fill the hearts of the poets with gladness or sorrow; always he longs for the beloved land of his fathers, and always his mind's eye is fixed on that land, which he addresses with all a lover's tenderness:

> Lovely land of song,
> With fruit and flowers vernal,
> Through all history's ages
> Thou art spring eternal.

Dolitzky's warm Zionist emotions found a powerful echo in the popular poems of Naphtali Herz IMBER (1856-1902), who was born in Galicia and was among the first settlers in Palestine. In 1886 he published in Jerusalem his first collection of poems, *Barkai*, in which he sings of the return to Zion, and of the new colonies then being founded in Palestine. These poems need revision; their language is not faultless or sufficiently poetical, but they are inspired by the spontaneous and unsophisticated love of a people for its ancestral land. They are not really the work of an individual poet: they are rather the creation of the populace, with which Imber was on a level in education and artistic taste. Poems of his like *The Hope* (*Hatikvah*) and *The Watch on the Jordan* have been set to simple tunes, and are widely sung in Palestine and elsewhere. *The Hope* has even been turned into the " national anthem" of the Zionist party. Its very simplicity is not ineffective:

> Our hope is not yet lost, our ancient hope of returning to the land of our fathers, to the city in which David encamped. . . .
> Brethren in the lands of my wandering, hearken to the voice of our Prophet: only with the last of the Jews will our hope perish.

A third poet, who died after an unhappy life at the age of twenty-seven, ranks far above both Dolitzky and Imber. This was Mordecai Zevi MANE (1860-1887). He was the son of a poor schoolmaster, and was educated in the Academy of Arts and Crafts at St. Petersburg, where one of his works was awarded a prize. A great future both as artist and poet was predicted for him, but death cut short his life, and only the poems and the essays on art which he left behind him testify to a great ability which was not given opportunity to develop. His poems betray the artist. Unlike most young poets, he wrote not a single love-poem; and unlike the majority of Hebrew poets who preceded him, he wrote no poem with a moral purpose. Two subjects, old yet ever new, engage his sorrowful muse: love of nature and the problem of suffering, that hidden, dumb suffering which enfolds all those young poets who know that their life on earth will not last long, that death is slowly but surely stealing upon them. In his last days a third motive, the love of Zion, was added to his strong love of nature and his consuming sorrow. For his single Zionist poem, *My Soul's Desire*, he weaves a harmonious pattern of his three themes: the longing for respite from his crushing private woes, the longing for life in the bosom of nature—the sweet peaceful nature of the new Judæa—and the hope of a national spiritual revival, closely linked with a material revival, which is to come as the result of healthy labour on the land:

> Sun of springtime westward soars,
>   To the borders of the skies;
> There its limpid glory pours,
>   A feast for thirsting eyes.
>
> All about, serene and still;
>   Not a leaflet flits
> Where in silence on a hill
>   Alone the poet sits.
>
> Ah, how pleasant is the spring;
>   Who can voice its art?
> Day to day of hope shall sing
>   For the human heart.
>
> The drooping spirit lives again,
>   And dreams of many things;
> Forgets its weariness, its pain,
>   And soars aloft on wings.
>
> All about, serene and still—
>   Hear now! Wings astir!
> Lightly breezes round me thrill,
>   Lightly branches stir.
>
> There the stork with outspread pinions,
>   Dazzling as white fire,
> Cleaving through the blue dominions,
>   Circles, rises higher.

Ah, were eagle's wings for me,
   That I, too, might soar!
Or at least as man is free
   Come and go once more!

Then I'd fly, I'd travel east,
   Where Halevi sang and died.
There how soon my pains had ceased
   In the fruitful countryside!

Holy land, where are you? Where?
   My spirit yearns for you!
My soul's life is in your air
   And my body's healing, too.

My soul's life is in your air,
   And for you my longing;
Visions holy, visions rare,
   In my dream come thronging.

Dazzling sunshine beams on earth,
   Dews of twilight glisten;
To farmers' singing strong with mirth
   From afar I listen.

From the brook a shepherd's flute
   Pipes his flocks to water,
While sweetly answers from the hut
   A song of Israel's daughter.

In that fruitful, blooming land,
   I would labour, too;
Labour, sing and breathe the air,
   Till strength might come anew!

I'd forget my grief, my sorrow,
   All my long repining;
Days of peace, a sweet to-morrow,
   Towards me still are shining.

Holy land, where are you? Whither?
   My spirit yearns for you;
Ah! that you and I together
   Might yet be born anew!

Mané's poetical style is simple and easy, without excessive ornament or word-play, and with a sad and appealing tenderness. He was one of the first to use European verse-rhythm in place of the eleven-syllable metre used by almost all the Hebrew poets before him.

The new tendencies in Hebrew thought found expression also in a new novel. Reuben Asher BRAUDES, who in the 'seventies wrote *Religion and Life*, published in 1888 a novel entitled *The Two Extremes*. It is an attempt to find a synthesis of orthodoxy and progress on a basis of nationalism. This novel, which is full of interest from the point of view of technique, describes an Odessa Jew, Ahitub, who spends some time on business in a small Lithuanian town. Ahitub belongs by social position and education to that well-to-do middle-class which has no interest in the Hebrew language and literature, and neglects the Jewish ceremonial laws, not out of conviction, but out of mere laxity. His wife Rosalie is given up to pleasure, and is absorbed entirely in fashions, dress and the social round, like most of the Jewish women of " high society," i.e. the moneyed " aristocracy." His sister Lisa is a romantic girl, beautiful and emotional, an accomplished pianist, but without any ideal in life or desire for a fuller existence; she finds satisfaction in the romantic dreams of a girl whose days pass by in boredom and idleness. Ahitub, brought up in this empty environment, suddenly comes into an entirely different world : a patriarchal Jewish family, soaked in tradition and deep-seated religious belief. It is not surprising that this quiet, deeply religious life, with the charm of a homely poetry which breathes vitality into the observance of the Jewish feasts and the performance of the Jewish rites, captures the heart of Ahitub, who has hitherto lived the restless, hurried life of the large town, surrounded by the empty, superficial glitter of a bourgeois environment. So when in this townlet, among Jews who are sincerely attached to their God and their people, he encounters the young and beautiful Shifrah, a simple and uneducated girl, but pure and unspoilt, whose life is not filled with the one desire to appear beautiful and attract attention, and who does not feed her imagination with love-scenes from the familiar type of French novel—he feels himself drawn to her.

But Ahitub soon sees not only the bright spots in the picture : he also has glimpses of the black shadows in the old Jewish manner of life. He observes how the orthodox persecute anyone who dares to hold an opinion on the pettiest religious question differing from the traditional view. He realises the narrow outlook of the people, the defects in their community organisation. And the question arises in his mind : Which is the better of the two? The newer Judaism, which has nothing specifically Jewish in it at all, or the older Judaism, which is so rich in content but so narrow and fanatical as to leave not a breath of fresh air?

Hezron, Shifrah's brother, travels to Odessa on the same business which brought Ahitub to stay at Hezron's father's house. Hezron, an orthodox provincial, makes the acquaintance of the specious, garish life of the wealthy Odessa Jews and gets to know Lisa, Ahitub's sister. Being a man of refined sensibility, he finds pleasure in the polite manners that prevail in Ahitub's wealthy father's house, in the fine comfortable furniture, the like of which he has never seen at home, and generally in the variety and hum of life in the large city; and in his heart he compares this new life with the old-fashioned life of his home-town, and comes to the conclusion that the existence which he and his parents lead is semi-barbarous in its poverty and monotony. His wife is certainly not ill-looking, but how she dresses! And what does she know, and what are her interests? Rosalie, Ahitub's wife, and his sister Lisa are very different: how beautiful and fine they are in their rich dresses, how at home Lisa is in literature, how well Lisa plays the piano, and how fluently she speaks foreign languages! Hezron likes everything that Ahitub has learnt to loathe, because Hezron has not yet seen all the ugly shadows in that life which is so brilliant on the outside. But it is certain that his enthusiasm will not be long-lived. The day will come when he too will realise that all that he sees in the rich house of the Odessa Jew is false, a mere mask, outward glamour with nothing behind.

Thus a sort of " Gordian knot " is tied, which is cut by a new hero who now appears on the stage, Hezron's grandfather, a *Maskil* of the period of Adam Hakohen and M. A. Günzburg, who combines all that is beautiful and noble in European civilisation with all that is good and valuable in the much older national culture of the Jewish people. The old life remains in essentials what it was, but it is more polished and more European. This is the "synthesis " reached by Braudes, his compromise between " the two extremes."

A similar view, elaborated into a system, is found in the work of the publicist and scholar Zev JAWITZ (1848-1924), an orthodox nationalist writer and disciple of Yehiel Michal Pines. He saw in the Jewish religion what Chateaubriand and Schleiermacher saw in Christianity. In the Jewish religion he finds no leaning towards asceticism or abstention from worldly pleasures, but on the contrary, an affirmative attitude to life, which, though it imposes on the Jew many burdensome religious and moral obligations, still makes Jewish life healthy and full of present happiness : for Jewish morality is a morality of this world, of national and social life. Although the Jewish religion bridles human passions, it does not stifle them completely, nor do its rules make demands which the ordinary Jew cannot fulfil. It affords full scope for whatever is good and useful, and only guards the Jew from debauchery, licentiousness and harmful excesses. Thus the observance of the numerous ceremonial rites and customs, though apparently a heavy yoke, is not a burden to the Jew who has not become assimilated to the Gentiles and does not try to imitate them. On the contrary, the ceremonial laws preserve the purity of his morals, fill his life with the poetry of religion, and bestow on him a satisfying sense of unity with his God, his people and mankind at large. In Jawitz's view, none of the beliefs and rules of the Jewish faith is antiquated: they none of them prevent a Jew from being thoroughly European in his habits and manners, or from being a useful member of modern society. Nor is European science, such as deserves the name, antagonistic to the Jewish faith. The supposed antagonisms exist only for the superficial observer, and are to be accounted for entirely by the excessive and extravagant freedom of thought which has filled science and philosophy with baseless theories. Zionism is an inseparable element in the Jewish religion, which has always been fundamentally national and " Palestinian." All that is needful is to purify the idea of Revival from the mischievous notions of those nationalists who are half sunk in assimilation.

True to this point of view, Jawitz wrote a *History of Israel* (1895-1924) in a strictly orthodox spirit, and retold in verse and prose the wonderfully poetical legends of the Talmud (*Sihoth minni Kedem*, 1887, and *Neginoth minni Kedem*, 1892); he also wrote sketches of the life of the Jewish colonists in Palestine, whom he described as young Jews, healthy in body and mind, who find the religious observances no burden but a pleasure and a joy. Jawitz, it may be added, ranks high as a Hebrew stylist; and though his ideas have exerted little influence on modern Hebrew literature, his style and his poetry have counted for a good deal.

In this fashion, then, Braudes and Jawitz find a compromise between Judaism and humanism, between the religion of Israel and modern civilisation. At bottom it is no compromise at all: it is pure conservatism, in which the concessions to modern life are only imaginary. The Jews, who have lived among other nations and have involuntarily and unconsciously been influenced by them, are not in need of a superficial adaptation to the outward forms of present-day civilisation, but of a thorough amalgamation of all the best and choicest of what they have inherited from their historic past with whatever is of the essence of modern humanistic culture. It is this deeper synthesis that was attempted by Asher GINZBERG (1856-1927), better known by his pen-name AHAD HA-AM (" One of the people ").

Ahad Ha-Am turned Zionism, which at first had been only a political ideal, into a national Jewish philosophy of life, embracing almost every aspect of Jewish life and action. He brought a wide range of knowledge and an acutely logical mind to the task of providing a philosophico-historical basis for Jewish nationalism and Zionism. This basis is to be found in a series of short and penetrating essays in the vein of popular philosophy, entitled *Perurim* (" Crumbs ").

In these essays Ahad Ha-Am, examining certain phases of the history of Judaism in the light of the teachings of sociology and folk-psychology, shows that the new nationalist movement in Judaism is no accident or passing phase. Zionism, or *Hibbath Zion* as it had previously been called, is an inevitable consequence of the course of Jewish history during the last few centuries, which was closly bound up with the main currents of general European life and thought. Zionism cannot therefore be regarded as a mere result of anti-Semitism; nor is it a political ideal only, or a mere economic enterprise. According to Ahad Ha-Am, "Zionism is not a part of Judaism, nor an addition to it: it is the whole of Judaism, but with a change of centre." Zionism is the spiritual concentration of the race on the idea of national survival and spiritual emancipation, which become possible only by the creation of a national historic centre in which Jews and Judaism can attain untrammelled development in conformity with their historical qualities and national habits, which have taken on new forms owing to the influence of the common civilisation of modern times. This is the core of Zionism, and this and this only can be attained in Palestine by a purposive colonisation, carried out gradually, cautiously and without impatience, and preferring quality to quantity. To this end cultural work in particular must be furthered both in Palestine itself and elsewhere, since only a minority of the Jewish people—a minority, however, that is more important than the majority if it be but a majority in relation to the rest of the people of Palestine*–can be confined within the historic mother-country of the Jewish race. At present a complete " in-gathering of all the exiles " is outside the bounds of possibility. Consequently Zionism cannot wholly solve the purely economic side of the Jewish problem (though it can of course create an independent national system of manufacture and commerce for the Jews in Palestine).

Ahad Ha-Am also thought it impossible to achieve the ultimate political object by diplomacy or political means, as imagined by Theodor Herzl. In his Zionist creed " the

*See *Al Parashath Derakhim*, II, **64-65** (Ed. 1921).

Jewish state is not the alpha, but the omega." Hence Ahad Ha-Am's Zionism is called " Spiritual Zionism." It is sharply opposed both to the purely practical *Hibbath Zion* that preceded Herzl, and to the " Political Zionism " of Herzl and Max Nordau. But this title, " Spiritual Zionism," does not do justice to the scope of Ahad Ha-Am's system. There is scarcely a single serious problem in any way affecting Jews and Judaism which Ahad Ha-Am has not dealt with and attempted to answer. Besides an important series of articles on problems of Palestinian colonisation and Jewish schools in Palestine, he wrote on the " spiritual nationalism " of Dubnow, and showed that a people without a territory could never secure complete national autonomy in the countries where it was in exile. He wrote on national ethics, showing that a nation's ethical standard ceases after a time to be dependent on its religion, and begins to exist independently and to conform with the general spiritual development reached by the nation. He wrote on " the transvaluation of values," and showed that Judaism also had the ideal of the " superman "; but this " superman " is not Nietzsche's " blonde beast," but " the hero of the spirit," one who is an extremist in his ethical standards and impatient of compromise in his fight for ethical values, and, like Ibsen's hero, Brand, cries " All or nothing!" More than this, by the sheer fact of its survival Judaism has created something in the nature of a further development of Nietzsche's ideas: a " supernation," which, too, is extremist and impatient of compromise, and therefore rightly calls itself " the chosen people "—chosen, however, not for worldly power, but to be the world's supreme type of a moral nation. He wrote an article entitled " Flesh and Spirit," in which he argues that Judaism does not aim " at mortifying the flesh for the sake of the spirit, but at exalting the flesh by means of the spirit." He wrote an article on the difference between Judaism and Christianity, in which he shows that Judaism has set its religio-ethical ideas within a framework of social legislation for the nation, and that it never indulged in mystical worship of a human being, nor reached that extreme altruism which is only " inverted egotism." He wrote on " Slavery in Freedom " and " Slavery in Revolution," and put forward the original idea that the Jews, though free in the religious, civil and political sense, are unconsciously enslaved to the nations that rule over them, or to those sects and parties with which the free-born Jews live and work, so that these " free men " are but slaves in spirit. Before a gathering of Russian Zionists at Minsk he delivered a lecture on " Culture " (later printed under the title " The Spiritual Revival "), in the course of which he touched on Hebrew art, which again loses greatly, not only from a nationalist, but also from a general human point of view, by becoming itself enslaved to strangers. He wrote an article on "The Language Struggle," dealing with the relation between Hebrew and Yiddish, in which he explains that even a language spoken by the people cannot become a national language unless it is wrapped up with that people's historical consciousness, since any other language would not include within it the essential qualities of a product of the nation's history. He wrote on " The Language and its Literature " and " The Language and its Grammar," dealing with the problem of creating new words and the purity of the Hebrew language, and expressing the opinion that only fresh and profounder thinking will help to enrich Hebrew with new words and to create new grammatical, stylistic and syntactical forms. He wrote a psychological sketch of Moses, expressing the idea that a legendary personality can, in the course of history, influence a people through the conception which they themselves have formed about it, no less than a real personality can influence them by actual achievements.

This is a brief summary of the problems dealt with by Ahad Ha-Am in his numerous articles (now collected in four volumes, entitled " At the Parting of the Ways," 1895-1913: new edition 1921), which were first printed in *Ha-Shiloah*, a monthly periodical which he founded in 1897 as a vehicle for the expression of these and like ideas. All these various ideas of his have exerted a profound influence on modern Hebrew literature. The greatest influence of all, however, was his central theme : that the core of the effort towards national revival must be " a living, heartfelt longing for national unity, for the revival of the nation and its development in accordance with its own spirit on the common basis of human civilisation."

At the end of the 'eighties, after the reaction following the pogroms had begun gradually to pass away, there had arisen an antagonism between two sets of ideas : the old ideas of the Maskilim of the 'seventies, who wanted radical changes and reforms in the Jewish religion and in Jewish social life, and the newer ideas of the nationalists and *Hovevé Zion*, who sought to keep alive the finer qualities of traditional Judaism. At the same time, the outlook for Jewish life in general was anything but reassuring. On the one side there were the orthodox masses, who venerated the dead letter, and whose real human emotions had congealed and hardened; on the other were the *intelligentsia*, who had lost all healthy national sentiment and love for the cultural heritage of the Jewish race and its national hopes. A people marked by " two extremes " such as these was incapable of beginning to create a complete and independent life. Certainly radical reforms were needed in Judaism, but not sudden and artificial reforms like those demanded during the 'seventies. In the opinion of Ahad Ha-Am it was impossible for a " negative " movement to create the positive social and ethical values which Judaism needed. These could be brought into being only by a vital longing for a revival, which must include a positive aspiration after free citizenship, such as had been lost to the Jews these two thousand years, and a negative attitude towards the petrified Judaism of the Ghetto. In order that this vitalising and invigorating ideal might have a firm basis, Judaism must have a national spiritual centre in Palestine, which in future would exert an influence over the Jews of all lands, and so help towards spiritual unity and revival, and later also towards political redemption.

But work in Palestine could not by itself suffice to bring about this revival : there must likewise be preparation in the lands of exile to meet the great coming changes in the spiritual and political condition of scattered Jewry. The Jewish nation needed to be raised intellectually and morally to a higher level, to be cleansed of a host of defects and failings that had become deeply rooted in the great body of the people as a result of Ghetto life, persecutions and restrictions. For the achievement of this great purpose of raising up a new generation, of renewing the nation in exile, Ahad Ha-Am proposes two principal means : education and literature. These two are needed gradually to root out not only the assimilationist tendencies of the Jewish *intelligentsia*, but also the weaknesses in the Jewish character which are the result of various historical causes. Ahad Ha-Am protests against the writers of the 'sixties and 'seventies, who persisted in fighting only against the specifically Jewish defects in the Jew, against the Jew that was in the man, and hardly paid any attention at all to his shortcomings as a human being, to the man that was in the Jew. The time had come when it should be understood that the object of the idea of Revival was to make the ideal of a rebirth at once national and human, the central rallying point of Jewish life.

This is Ahad Ha-Am's synthesis. But this synthesis between Judaism and humanism was still imperfect. In Ahad Ha-Am's writings one feels that the scale is weighted on the side of Judaism. That the synthesis might be perfect and that there might afterwards arise out of it the complete fusion of the "eternally human" with the "absolutely spiritual" in Judaism, it was necessary to incline the scale to the other side, the side of common humanism. Such a tendency can be recognised in the work of many writers who followed Ahad Ha-Am, and who will be dealt with in the next chapter.

But even before the advent of Ahad Ha-Am, this tendency had been exhibited by the critic, poet and novelist David FRISCHMANN (1863-1922), the first " European " in Hebrew literature. Before Frischmann almost all Jewish writers had been more or less " theologians " in a negative or positive sense : they had either defended or attacked the Jewish religion. Frischmann had one single ideal—humanism. He was an anti-Zionist, and in some sense (in his earlier writings) an anti-nationalist, because he feared that Zionism and nationalism might lead to chauvinism and stifle humanism in the Jew. While the Hebrew writers of the 'sixties and 'seventies wrote or translated books on subjects of general human interest as a means of increasing "enlightenment" among the Jews, Frischmann wrote or translated similar books without any such ulterior object. For him their human interest was an end in itself, in Hebrew just as in any other living language and literature.

Frischmann fought against the characteristic Jewish *batlanuth*, against the absurd euphuistic style and the ludicrous use of scraps of Biblical phraseology. He endeavoured, also, to bring the younger generation of Jews closer to nature, to give them a better appreciation of art, of belles-lettres, of woman, and, in general, to educate them on the aesthetic side. Until his time all the stress had been laid on the moral education of the Jew, and scarcely a thought had been given to his aesthetic education. In his *Letters on*

Literature Frischmann wields a broom (at times too vigorously, as in his brutal witticisms at the expense of Smolenskin, and his harsh comments on Lilienblum) to sweep away all the refuse which had accumulated in modern Hebrew literature. Sometimes among the refuse he sweeps away such artistic pearls as Peretz's poems; but as a rule he throws out only the scum, only what is pointless and tasteless. He prefers beauty of form to depth of subject-matter, but probably this was essential in the 'eighties as an antidote: for a long time past lack of form or indifference to form had been the rule in Hebrew literature.

Frischmann also wrote short stories and sketches (*The Three that Ate, Let him Remember*, and a series of *Flying Letters*) remarkable for their delicate psychological analysis and their beauty of form, even if their topics are not always original.

Modern Hebrew literature gained a novelist of the highest rank when it was rejoined by S. J. ABRAMOVITZ, who, in 1868, had published the novel *Fathers and Sons*. After that, until 1886, this writer (who called himself MENDELE MOCHER SEFARIM) wrote almost exclusively in Yiddish; but after 1886 he not only wrote new stories in Hebrew, but also translated into Hebrew his outstanding Yiddish stories—*My Mare, The Travels of Benjamin the Third, The Vale of Weeping*, and *In those Days*. His translations are themselves new works: his old Yiddish compositions, when retold in Hebrew, become entirely new. Mendelé virtually created a new Hebrew language. He began to make regular and systematic use of the very practical, concise and exact language of the Mishnah and the Midrash—unlike (for example) Gordon, whose prose writings are a bizarre patchwork of Biblical and Talmudic phraseology. He was the first of modern Hebrew writers to discard almost entirely the flowery Biblical style, which is unsuited to modern requirements. More than this, he introduced into modern Hebrew a unity of style not hitherto found even in the most realistic Hebrew writers. Thus on the linguistic side Mendelé Mocher Sefarim led the way for such supreme stylists as Bialik, Judah Steinberg and S. Ben-Zion.

Great, however, as is Mendelé's importance for the development of language and style, he played an even more decisive part in developing the technique of the modern novel It may be said without hesitation that he created an entirely new genre in Hebrew literature. He gave up the romantic tale with its love complications, which had served as a peg for the novels of Mapu, Smolenskin and Braudes. His novels and sketches are conceived on the " epic " scale. The plot is but a thread to link up the several chapters; each chapter is a veritable poem, an episode complete and rounded in itself. His work in general may be described as an artistic presentation of history—the living history of Russian Judaism from the 'forties to the 'eighties, before the great disintegration began in the patriarchal life of the Jews of Russia and Poland. At the time described by Mendelé, the life of all these Jews was of a piece: the patriarchal manner of life, which during centuries had become crystallised into a single type, embraced every side of the Jew's being in its rigid strength. This clearly defined manner of life Mendelé embodied in types which are composite, representative of a whole social order, rather than individual. Each of these types seems to be hewn out of pure marble. A single exclamation or momentary gesture reveals a whole world of feeling and thought. Mendelé's way of telling his story is so objective and free from psychological probing and analysis, that his description of life has the quality of plastic art. He is not only a painter but a sculptor. In his stories every single motion of the body is expressive of some mental emotion. No other author has painted a picture of the " Jewish quarter " so complete, so all-inclusive and so much " in the round." Not only has he painted the Jews of the " quarter"; the Christians with whom the Jews come in contact, and the very domestic animals and poultry, inseparable features of the " Jewish quarter," are painted in with Mendelé's spacious, unhurried brush. His epic calm and spaciousness place this annalist of the dingy Ghetto in the same category as the creators of the national epics of other races, which have drawn their inspiration directly from the immortal artistic legacy of ancient Greece. Yet this " Hellenist in spirit " is, in his own words, " a Jew of the Jews."

Sometimes he turns aside and finds relief in lyrical outpourings, which bring to mind the noblest passages in the Psalms. There is a notable example in *My Mare*. His descriptions of natural scenery show the consummate art of a poet who was in constant and intimate communion with nature. But with him even nature takes on a peculiar Jewish tinge, as though it had turned Jew. The trees of the forest in winter, covered with snow and swaying in the wind, are for him the swaying worshippers in the synagogue, wrapped in their fringed praying-shawls. Trees in the garden after rain are children being washed and combed by a loving mother on the Sabbath eve. Such similes abound. Through his combination of Judaism with Hellenism, of native Hebrew genius with supreme artistic achievement, this great depicter of Russian Jewry became the prince of Hebrew novelists, and the ultimate fount of inspiration of the more recent literature.

CHAPTER VI
THE MORE RECENT LITERATURE

"A living, heartfelt longing" and "free development on the common basis of human civilisation" are the underlying ideas that have chiefly influenced the development of recent Hebrew literature. Instead of "novels with a purpose" we get pure works of art, which seek to give an actual picture of the human being that is inside the Jew and to embody the psychological processes which, though they have a Jewish setting, are common to humanity.

In 1891 BEN AVIGDOR (Abraham Leib SHALKOVITCH, 1866-1921) began to publish a new series of novels under the general title *Sifré Agorah* ("Penny Books"). Ben Avigdor complained of the lack of artistry in Hebrew belles-lettres. All the novels were novels with a purpose and lacked naturalness. Their authors were always busy with argument and interminable philosophising. It was extremely rare to find true descriptions of life or real popular types. The writers did not realise the poetry of commonplace Jewish life—the piety, the patience under adversity, the extraordinary idealism of the simplest Jew, who, out of his abounding love, is ready to sacrifice everything for his God and his religion, and the pure family life, with its unparalleled wealth of affection and warm-heartedness. It was to these qualities of heart that the Jews owed their preservation in exile; but the propagandists of *Haskalah* had been blind to all this. Their "realism" had made them see folly and superstition in whatever failed to fit in with their limited "commonsense" outlook.

Ben Avigdor, therefore, with the aid of other writers, tried to present "positive" types drawn from ordinary Jewish life. He portrayed "Leah the Fishwife" (1891) with her poverty and her deep devotion to her meek, sickly husband, who knew nothing except the Gemara; the seamstress Deborah (in the story *Love and Duty*, 1892), who sacrifices her love, her one happiness, for the benefit of her poor parents, who are dependent on her scanty wages; and "The Happy Poor" (1893), who have nothing in their material world and need nothing—"joyful beggars" they, whose homes never lack peace and quiet or healthy Jewish humour. In his sketch *Menahem the Scribe* (1893), which made a great impression in its day, Ben Avigdor reproves the reactionaries and euphuistic phrasemongers among the nationalist Hebrew writers, and draws a distinction between nationalist and chauvinist literature.

In his historical novel *Four Hundred Years Ago* (1892) he describes Jewish life in Spain immediately before the expulsion, and the expulsion itself (1492). The hero, Don

Miguel, a crypto-Jew who deserts his sweetheart Clara, a Christian, because he does not wish to be parted from his brethren in their coming exile; his sister Emilia, consumed with deadly hatred towards her people's oppressors; the tutor Pereira, who, in his last hour, explains to his pupil Miguel that a race like the Jews, with so glorious a past and hopes for so glorious a future, has no right to commit suicide by assimilation, and in fact cannot become submerged in the gentile world and pass out of existence—all this was something quite new in Hebrew literature. It was a consequence of "the living, heartfelt longing" for a new national life, more complete and more human.

The longing for "free development on the common basis of human civilisation" served also—perhaps contrary to Ahad Ha-Am's idea or intention—as an impetus to the rise of enthusiastic advocates of a general humanistic literature in Hebrew, not as a means of propagating the ideal of "enlightenment," but as an end in itself, as the actual "enlightenment" itself, and as a main and essential part of Hebrew literature, to which it was as necessary as to any other living European literature. This view was put forward in an article entitled *Literature and Life*, by Zalman EPSTEIN (b. 1860), an essayist with a touch of poetic fire, who wrote attractive sketches of the life of Jews of the older generation. In this demand for a widening of the limits of Hebrew literature he was followed by Reuben BRAININ (b. 1863), author of biographies of Mapu and Smolenskin, a detailed study of Judah Löb Gordon, and many other literary and general essays. After Ben Yehuda he was the first to found a Hebrew literary organ devoted as much to topics of common human interest as to specifically Jewish subjects. His monthly " From East and West " (of which only four numbers appeared, 1894-1899) included articles on Tolstoy (by Abgad Ha-Edrei), on Nietzsche (by David Neumark), on Helmholtz (by Brainin), on " The Power of Life " (by Hermann Shapira), on agriculture (by Joseph Halévy), a translation of De Maupassant's *Le Horla*, and the like. In the opinion of Brainin and his colleagues, Hebrew literature had ceased to be a temporary medium for the spread of *Haskalah*, or even for introducing nationalist ideas to that section of the Jewish public which read Hebrew : it had become a living and all-embracing popular literature, designed, like any other modern European literature, to satisfy the requirements of its readers as cultured human beings, and not merely their requirements as Jews.

Many other writers championed this view of Hebrew literature : M. J. Berdichevsky (1865-1921), M. Ehrenpreis (b. 1869), a gifted critic and stylist, and others. They advocated this view in *Ha-Shiloah*, in opposition to its editor, Ahad Ha-Am, who himself held that while there was need for such a literature, the time for it was not yet. From this time onwards many books on subjects of general interest were translated into Hebrew from most European languages, and a fair number of original books on such subjects were written in Hebrew. These were mostly published by the "Tushiyah" publishing company, founded by Ben Avigdor. The earlier "Ahiasaf" company issued books of specifically Jewish interest (with the exception of Lippert's *History of Human Culture*, translated by David Frischmann, and Herbert Spencer's *Education*, translated by J. L. DAVIDOVITCH (Ben David)).

Shortly afterwards original poetical works of a "humanistic" character began to appear in Hebrew. Among these mention should be made of a small collection of poems by J. L. PERETZ (1851-1915), entitled *The Organ*. It includes only a few love-poems, but they express much that is deep and tender, and their craftsmanship is very pleasing. Here, for example, is his description of the lover's complaint:

> A murmur of my song was torn
> Sighing from my lyre's strings,
> And by a still small wind was borne
> To the world's ends on its wings.
>
> It flew—and when the river heard
> Its ripples wrung their hands and cried.

It flew—and when the forest heard
   With shrieks its trembling leaves replied.
It fluttered over hill and vale;
   The flowers saddened where it came,
And its own sister lily, pale,
   Inclined her head with shame.
It soared above the topmost wind:
   The stars for me entreated, throbbing.
It pierced the tent of heaven, to find
   The ministering angels sobbing.

—or a metaphorical description of a lover's enslavement to the emblem of his love:

The river preened itself and boasted of its crystal waters. " Within me," it said, " are the stars, and in my midst are the curtains of Heaven outstretched."

Suddenly the heavens above were covered, for storm-clouds had arisen, and now its skies were veiled and its lights extinguished, and the proud river was troubled.

—or this original lover's lament:

The heavens are dark as clods, and my soul droops, for soon clods of earth will cover my eyes. Now the clouds weep cold raindrops for my sorrow; anon my fair one's eyes will weep cold tears over my grave.

But Peretz the poet was surpassed by Peretz the story-teller. Not only in Yiddish literature, but also in Hebrew, he is the originator of the short, compact artistic literary sketch, the fine, delicate description, the symbolical story, and the allegorical legend. In addition to his Yiddish work, which was translated into Hebrew by himself, or with his help and under his supervision, he wrote *ab initio* in Hebrew a number of sketches and impressions noteworthy alike for their artistic beauty and their poetical conception, such as *Modern Melodies, Night of Terror, In a Summer House, The Thought and the Violin, The Hero Shemaiah, Four Precious Stones, Four Generations—Four Deaths, Getting Less,* and several plays, *The Fall of the Tzaddik's House, In Depression,* and others. In all these beautiful pieces the vivid poetic idea suddenly shines out like a flash of lightning, and an admirable terseness is combined with an original and attractive form. Peretz knew the heart of the Jewish masses, sympathised with their sufferings, and described their poverty and their hopes. He knew the heart of the Jewish woman and her pitiful and endlessly painful life (*Mistress Hannah*); he knew, too, the spiritual struggle of the intellectual Jew, and in several of his stories described this type, with its emptiness of heart, and its longing after the distant Jewish past, its yearning for which is intensified by estrangement. The popular studies which he entitled *From the Mouth of the People* are treasuries of legends enveloped in the charm of Jewish folklore, whose original and genuinely national flavour has not yet staled. His play, *The Fall of the Tzaddik's House,* and the series of hasidic stories (*Between Two Mountains, Whose House is Filled with Joy, The Soul of the Hasidim, The Transmutation of a Melody*, and the like) have kept alive all the valuable elements latent in Hasidism, which was the special contribution of Judaism to the 18th century—a movement which sprang from the heart of the people as a protest against the deadening hardness of rabbinic Judaism, against the stifling of living religion by the mass of dry ceremonial laws, against the decay of the joyous, uplifting service of God and its replacement by routine observance and arid Talmudic casuistry. Generally speaking, if Mendelé Mocher Sefarim is the ultimate source of inspiration of the newer Hebrew literature, Peretz is its immediate source; for by his attempt to show what was illuminating in Hasidism, Peretz raised up a generation of Hebrew writers who portrayed Hasidism in glowing, tender colours, and thus inspired affection for this religious movement, which the *Maskilim* had accounted the very source of ignorance and superstition. One of these writers was Micah Joseph BERDICHEVSKY (1865-1921), who, besides drawing attractive pictures of the life of the Hasidim, found also, together with Hillel ZEITLIN (b. 1872), a theoretical and poetic basis for Hasidism. Even more remarkable sketches of Hasidic life were written by Judah STEINBERG (1863-1908), an original and exceptionally skilful artist, in whom were many gleams of the spirit of Peretz.

The more this humanistic tendency increased in the newer school of literature, the more did the foremost writers penetrate to the roots of the Jewish problem. General human culture tends to supplant Jewish culture. The Jews are not an independent, self-sufficing race; both economically and culturally they depend on the peoples among whom they live. Hence they have no choice but to adapt themselves to the culture of those peoples. But if this process goes on unchecked, the day cannot be far distant when the cultural wealth of this four-thousand-year-old nation will be buried under the dust of museums. Now the distinctive culture of the Jews has created national values of great worth, and no Jew could reconcile himself to the idea that these should be allowed to perish from the world. But without a national culture no nation, bereft of a territory and a common language, can survive. Are the Jews, then, at the beginning of the end?

On the other hand, it is impossible for Judaism not to adapt itself to European culture: the " spiritual Ghetto " is just as narrow and hedged-in as the physical Ghetto. Historic Judaism contains much that is antiquated, many ideas and beliefs, inherited from the Middle Ages, which no thinking Jew could possibly accept.

Thus the nationally-minded Jew lives in two worlds, by each of which he is attracted, and the result is that lack of spiritual wholeness in the educated Jew, that duality and half-and-halfness which makes him defective both as Jew and as European. If he neither knows nor cares for his people, he becomes an undifferentiated human being without a national basis; if he knows his nation and cares for its spiritual possessions, he is weighed down by the tragedy of an ancient people, once militantly creative, now retreating and leaving to other races the eternal struggle in which it has held its own for so many generations.

This is the profound tragedy described by the short-lived novelist Mordecai Zevi FEIERBERG (1874-1898) in his sketches *The Amulet* and *The Shadows*, and especially in his brief symbolical story *At Evening*, and his long novel *Whither?*. In Feierberg's works, as in Berdichevsky's, the infinite sorrow of the nation is ever present. A nation with so glorious a past, a nation of saints and martyrs, unconquered by the pressure of Greek civilisation and the fires of the Inquisition—has it not strength enough to withstand the tide of modern life and civilisation? Feierberg puts into the mouth of Nahman, the hero of *Whither?*, his reply to this burning question. The Jews must return to their own land, but not merely to escape from persecution, but to lay there the foundations of a new society, a new life: not a shrivelled, harassed Jewish society like that in the Diaspora, but a live, healthy, upstanding

Jewish society, which shall yet again become a model for the whole world, as of old, and shall give to the whole world, and especially to the East, new life and aspirations and hopes, and a stimulus to new activities.

This was Feierberg's positive ideal. It combines the "Jewish" and the "human" elements: it demands a national revival "on the common basis of human civilisation" in the spirit of Ahad Ha-Am, whose fervent disciple Feierberg remained throughout his short life.

But Ahad Ha-Am also had opponents, of whom the most important was BERDICHEVSKY. In a series of essays he tried to introduce into Hebrew literature entirely new ideas about Israel's future cultural development. He adopted Nietzsche's view of Judaism—that it stands for asceticism and mortification of the flesh in the name of the spirit, in the name of theistic morality ("slave-morality" in Nietzsche's words). Like Nietzsche, Berdichevsky argues that the extreme universalism of the Prophets, their abstract spirituality and their exacting morality, sapped the nation's political vigour, ruined ancient Judæa materially, and, through the medium of Christianity, imposed on the whole world the heavy yoke of this ascetic moral code, and throttled whatever was natural and healthy in human passions and instincts, thus diminishing mankind's joy in life and hindering the advent of the highest human type, the "superman." Judaism had thus destroyed the nation's vigour even in the time of the Prophets. The Pharisees, and the Tannaim after them, though innocent of the universalist tendencies of the Prophets, still suffered from their exaggerated spirituality, and the Academy of Jamnia counted more for them than the political life for which Jerusalem stood. Jeremiah had destroyed Judæa's political freedom in the time of the first Temple; Rabbi Jochanan ben Zakkai destroyed the national freedom in the time of the second.

This is a new form of the attitude towards the Prophets and Tannaim which appears in J. L. Gordon's poem *Zedekiah in Prison*. Berdichevsky elaborates this point of view. He shows that for two thousand years Judaism has swallowed up the Jews: in other words, religion and morality have crushed all desire for a natural and healthy life, and an exaggerated spirituality has banished all the political aspirations which are essential to national existence. Even if the Jews should now gain political freedom in Palestine, the abstract Jewish religion and the exaggerated spirituality of the Jews would soon destroy it. Therefore, in Nietzsche's phrase, the Jews must "transvaluate all values." Jews must be preferred to Judaism. The Jews must lead a natural, earthly, material existence. The House of Israel must become "like all the nations";

then only will it be fit for a political revival as a live and healthy people.

Berdichevsky is thus an outright opponent of the "Spiritual Zionism" of Ahad Ha-Am, who held that the Jews must remain what they were, " a people of the spirit "; and in his stories Berdichevsky depicts healthy types of " earthly " Jews of the older generation, over against younger Jews who suffer from duality and lack of wholeness, who have ceased to follow historic Judaism, yet have not attained to European culture (as in his long stories, *Two Camps* and *It Ends in Smoke*, and many short stories). Berdichevsky was also one of the first " decadents " and " modernists " in Hebrew literature. His stories and articles did much to revolutionise the entire literature, in spite of their extremism and *outré* character and their many inconsistencies, and in spite of his curious language, which is compounded of Bible, Mishnah, Midrash and even the cabbalistic Zohar.

Even more extreme than Berdichevsky was S. I. HOROWITZ (1860-1922), who, in his essays *On the Survival of Judaism, Extending the Bounds*, and others, went so far as to abolish the dividing line between Judaism and non-Judaism, thus approaching a denial of the right of Judaism to survive at all. In his essays on *Rabbi Judah Ha-Levi, Hasidism and Haskalah*, and the like (in the annual *He-Atid* which he issued in 1908 and the following years) he objects to the emphasis on specifically Jewish national characteristics in the poems and philosophy of Judah Ha-Levi, in the Hasidism of Baal Shem Tob, in the spiritual teaching of Ahad Ha-Am, and elsewhere.

An original view of the differences between Judaism and Hellenism was introduced by the Jewish philosopher David NEUMARK (1866-1924), author of *The Problem of Freewill in the Works of Kant and Schopenhauer*, *The Philosophy of Judah Ha-Levi*, and, especially, *World Outlook and the Outlook on Life* (1903). In this last essay, Neumark argues that a " world-outlook " is acquired by a man's observation of the outer world that surrounds him, and " an outlook on life " when a man limits his observation to his own inner world. The former comes from outside, and concentrates its attention on nature; hence it creates the science of logic, philosophy, the natural sciences, the plastic arts and dramatic or epic poetry. The latter springs from within, and is specially concerned with man and his soul; hence it creates psychology, sociology, religion, lyric poetry, and music. The bent of Judaism (also found exceptionally in non-Jews) has been mainly towards the creation of values of the latter category, while that of Hellenism (also found exceptionally among Jews) has been to create values of the former category; and the conflict between these two tendencies of the human spirit has enriched not only humanity at large, but also Judaism, because in the more recent period, as a result of outside influences, it has gone on within Judaism itself.

These two tendencies, the spiritual-nationalist and the secular-nationalist, which respectively found expression in the writings of Ahad Ha-Am and of Berdichevsky, find their counterparts in the works of the two outstanding Hebrew poets of to-day, Haim Nahman BIALIK and Saul TCHERNICHOVSKY.

Bialik (b. 1873) is a national Hebrew poet both in content and in form. Ancient Hebrew poetry reaches its highest level only when it is primarily lyrical—that is to say, when it expresses the poet's personal and subjective feelings, which become common property only because of their depth and human appeal. The Psalms, the Lamentations of Jeremiah, and the bitter plaints of Job, are distinguished mainly for their profound lyrical quality. They appeal to us to-day because the expression of their emotions issues from the depth of a suffering Jewish heart, whose individual sorrow is merged in the sorrow of its people and the sorrow of the world. But in plastic form and the artistic delineation of the outer world —the two main foundations of the epic poem —Hebrew poetry is much inferior to Greek and even to Hindu poetry. Bialik is, first of all, a lyric poet, and in this quality he has

few equals even in other literatures. The
force and impulsiveness of his lyrical passion,
the freshness and spontaneity of his emotion,
are unmatched in Hebrew literature. His
intense introspection gives to his poems their
tremendous emotional appeal. His love-
poems are no more than a craving for love,
and his " Songs of Splendour " (*Shiré ha-
Zohar*) are the cry of one dazzled by the
sunlight which he has never seen before : his
description of sunlit scenes is not plastic and
objective, but emotional and subjective.
Hence there is no sense of proportion in his
" Songs of Splendour "; he is too profuse.
Even his narrative poems, except " The Dead
of the Desert," are more lyrical than epic :
they are deficient in action, which is the
primary requisite in an epic poem, and con-
sist mostly of emotional outpourings and
rapturous descriptions of nature. " Splendour " and " The Pool," which are simply
a string of disconnected pictures of great
beauty—and still more *Ha-Matmid*—are
fundamentally lyric poems. " In The City of
Slaughter " (" The Burden of Nemirov ")
is a " burden " in the true prophetic sense.
Even in " The Scroll of Fire," which is
to a great extent genuinely descriptive and
narrative, the lyric element predominates
markedly over the epic (it may suffice to mention " The Song of Perdition," and " The
Confession "). But it is precisely as a
lyric poet that Bialik comes nearer in spirit

to Judaism than any other Hebrew poet; and in this sense he has rightly been acclaimed as *the* national poet of his generation.

Not only in the quality of his poetic gift is Bialik genuinely national, but also in his subject-matter. The poems of his first ten years (1891-1901) breathe an unbounded love for the ancient Judaism of the Bible and the Talmud, a mighty yearning for the treasures of Judaism pure and undefiled, which are gradually perishing through force of present-day circumstances and through the spiritual feebleness of the Jews of to-day—the same love and yearning which we find in Feierberg. In his *On the Threshold of the House of Study*, he styles the Jewish Beth ha-Midrash—in which more studying than praying is done, and which the "enlightened" Jews of the 'seventies considered the root of all evil—"the hiding-place of the abiding spirit" and "the refuge of the eternal people." Only through this "House of Study" did "Israel save its God and God save His people." In his poem *If Thou Wouldst Know*, Bialik likens the Beth ha-Midrash to a spring from which his down-trodden brethren during evil times drew strength and courage to go forth rejoicing to meet death, "to bare the neck to every unsheathed knife and every upraised axe," to mount the stake, to leap into the fire and, with their creed on their lips, die the death of saints. He likens it to a spring, from which his oppressed brethren " in the straits of hell and the depths of the pit and among scorpions, draw divine consolation, confidence, steadfastness, patience, and iron strength to bear all hardship, with shoulder bent to endure a life of despite and contempt," to suffer endlessly, unboundedly and without hope of coming respite. He likens it to a place in which Israel has hidden its choicest treasure, its Law, to " the bosom in which have been poured all the people's tears and heart and soul and bitterest grief," and to a house filled with divine consolation, which has heartened the children of Israel in its faith in the Messiah.

But with Bialik this strong love for the source of the national religion which is Judaism soon becomes a tragic love—a romantic love for something doomed to extinction. Bialik loves Judaism with the devoted attachment of a child of the 'eighties; but like a child of the 'seventies he also realizes that in these days there is no purpose in the devotion of hundreds and thousands of young Jews to lifeless studies. The conflict in the poet's soul between these opposing emotions finds expression in his fine lyric poem *Ha-Matmid*.

A young *Yeshivah* student spends all his days and nights studying the Talmud and its commentaries. The peculiar melancholy sing-song in which the disputations of the Talmud are recited induces sad thoughts in the poet.

The *Matmid*, the "persistent student," has nothing in the world but the Gemara. The pleasures of life are utterly strange to him. Not for him does the lily bloom or the nightingale sing. He knows nothing of the grandeur of nature or the sweetness of love. Even the poetry of the Bible is not for him. Yet he is still a human being with a living soul; nay more, he has the soul of an idealist, tender and impressionable, prepared to sacrifice itself on the altar of "Torah." His heart knows the tumult of passion; he, too, feels drawn by the wonderful magic of a summer night, the wide fields and the sweet scent of pastures and meadows; he, too, has ambition, and craves for freedom and love and all the pleasures of this life. But he smothers all these urgent claims of the young heart and offers himself as a sacrifice—on whose altar? On the altar of the dead letter, of antiquated disputations and casuistries which have nothing to do with the life of the present day. How terrible it is, how tragic! With the artist's pen Bialik portrays the ferment that goes on in the sorrow-laden heart of the *Matmid*, whose unhappy fate is bound up with the unnatural life of a people that is homeless and without a national soil beneath its feet—a people that has been robbed of all earthly joys, and has thereby been forced to nourish itself exclusively on spiritual food, on food from heaven.

One of the finest of his shorter poems,

Alone, breathes a still more intense yearning for the ancient Judaism that is now perishing:

> The wind bore them all off, the light snatched them all away, a new song filled the morn of their life with melody; while I, a tender young dove, was utterly forgotten beneath the wings of the *Shechinah*.
>
> Lonely, lone I was left . . . and the *Shechinah*, too, set her broken right wing atrembling upon my head. My heart knew her heart: she was sore troubled for me, her only son. . . .
>
> Already had she been driven out of every corner; but there was still one tiny desolate hiding-place left her—the House of Study . . . . There she covered herself in the shadow and I joined her in her affliction.
>
> And when my heart failed with longing for the window, for the light, and when the space beneath her wing was strait for me, she leant her head against my shoulder and her tears fell upon the open page of my *Gemara*.
>
> She wept silently because of me and clung to me, and seemed to spread out her broken wing over me. "The wind has borne them all off, they have all flown away, and I am left alone, alone. . . ." It was like to the close of a very ancient dirge, like to a prayer of pleading and of fear, that I heard in that subdued weeping, in that hot tear. . . .

"The close of a very ancient dirge," "a prayer of pleading and of fear"—yes: to the landless Jewish people, without a common language, without a common government, the survival of the *Beth ha-Midrash* is not merely a subject for romantic sentiment, but a matter of life and death. Nineteen hundred years has the *Beth ha-Midrash* preserved the Jews from extinction; now it is on the point of death; what can take its place? With it will perish also the uniqueness of Jewry, its distinctiveness from all other peoples, with their different ways of life. On what, then, will the nation live in its scattered condition? This uniqueness, this " splendid isolation " of one people among all the other peoples of the world, is portrayed in Bialik's classic poem *The Dead of the Desert*.

The " dead " sleep in the terrible desert of exile, sunk deep in the sand of restrictions and ceremonial laws, without any sign of life. Yet these dead men are indeed giants, who even in their seeming death can strike terror into the " lords of the desert." An eagle in search of prey alights on them—

> The giant child of the rocks, with hooked beak and curved talons, it makes ready to drive its irresistible claws into the adamant breast. The sharp beak is poised above the flinty face . . . yet a moment, and the eagle will pounce on the body, and iron will grate upon iron. . . .

But the eagle starts back in fright: it is beyond his strength to pierce the flint, hardened during four thousand years. A " speckled snake, one of the fiery serpents of the wilderness " comes sneaking and crawling towards the giants, to hiss its poison at them. But it also turns back, " frightened by their quiet majesty." Then there comes a lion "mighty in power," an age-long dweller in the desert—

> The lion stands amazed at the grandeur of slumbering might—suddenly the lion shakes his mane and roars: and for leagues on untold leagues around the wastes of the desert are shaken.

But even the lion is forced to turn away before the "slumbering magnificence" of the corpses in the desert. No onslaught from above—religious persecutions—and no hissing of serpents from beneath—religious slanders and bribes—nor even direct assault—oppressions and restrictions and exactions—can destroy the seeming corpses—the "Valley of dry bones" which Ezekiel beheld in his vision.

> Yet anon the desert awakes in hatred of the eternal silence, and rouses itself to be avenged once for all on its Maker for its desolation.

And then the "dead of the desert," "dowered with overwhelming strength, mighty in terror," awake and no longer endure their harsh lot, the lot of endless exile. They arise and proclaim that they "are the last generation of oppression and the first of redemption;" then come great "Messianic movements," like that of Shabbethai Zevi, in which Israel arouses itself to new life, and revolts against God and His Law—for in time of Messianic movements the Law is annulled and all is permitted. But this rebellion against the power on high does not last long. Again the desert sand covers up the doughty giants; but they still remain a source of fear to those that hate them, and no man is able to make an end of them. Such is the Jewish people, which, like a " living mummy," has endured by the strength of Judaism through two thousand years in the terrible desert of exile.

But while Bialik admires the soundheartedness and stiff-neckedness of the exiled Jews before the era of emancipation, he has nothing but contempt for the half-and-half Jews of this generation, who lack the strength either to affirm their Judaism or wholly to deny it, and always stand in fear of " what the gentiles will say." To such spiritually-enfeebled Jews Bialik becomes a sternly rebuking and reproving prophet. His admiration for the whole-hearted Jew of earlier ages, in whom he sees something great and sublime, is matched by the indignation provoked in him by the Jew of the present day. A few days before the First Zionist Congress (1897) he voiced his complaint against his people in a veritable prophetic arraignment:

Verily the people is grass, it is dry as wood!
Verily the people is a corpse, heavy beyond belief!
For though the voice of God thunder on this side and on that, yet the people moves not nor stirs, nor quivers, nor rises lion-like. Nay, not even one man in a city bestirs him at the call, nor doth the heart of all the people tremble together for glad-

ness from the East and West and from sea unto sea, when its sons return to it, the seed of the living God, come from afar at the voice of the Lord. No hand is outstretched, no greeting given to all who call on His name in faith and trust. Amid the clamour of a foolish people round golden idols, the voice of God is hidden and His mighty thunder swallowed up. And with witless, wicked heart and reproach and contempt they despise the word of the Lord and make of it a laughing stock.

Verily the people is withered, debased, foul and corrupt from the sole of the foot to the head! For on a day of sickness and pain they have not raised from their midst a master of deeds, a living man with a beating heart, and in his heart a spark to fire the blood, and on his head a star to illumine the way of the people; a man to whom the name of the people and its God shall be more precious than wealth and gold, those false idols; in whom there shall be little pride of heart, much truth and power, a mighty hatred of a life of contemptible slavery, pity great as the sea, compassion manifold as the sufferings of his hapless people and as its heavy yoke; who shall hear the cry clamouring in his heart, clamouring and tossing like the sea, flaming like fire, flaming and kindling his blood, thundering, echoing ceaselessly, by day and by night: "Rise up and work, rise up and do, for the hand of God is with us!"

Verily the people is lost, contemptible, abject; its works have no foundation, its actions no measure. Millenia of wandering, exile insufferable, have perverted the heart, have dulled the nation's wit. Schooled to bear the rod and the whip, can they feel the pain, the shame of the soul that suffers, apart from the scourging of the body? A people that grovels in the valley of Exile darker than the Pit—can it take thought for the morow? Can it possess its soul till dawn and prophesy the sunrise, mark out its course to a distant end, and plan for a generation? No: it will not awake save the whip waken it, will not arise save violence constrain it. The fallen leaf, the hyssop that grows in the dust-heap, the withered vine, the faded shoot—can dew revive these? And when the trumpet sounds and the banner is unfurled, will the dead move? will the dead stir?

This famous poem exhibits all the great qualities of Bialik and also all his defects: prophetic pathos, emotional vigour, a rich and forceful style, but at the same time excessive length and lack of a sense of proportion.

Still more awe-inspiring in matter and more harshly reproving, but more polished and finished in manner, is the poem *This too is God's Chastisement*, which Bialik wrote in 1905, at the time of the Russian emancipation movement, when the younger generation of Russian Jews for the most part threw themselves into the general struggle:

Verily this too is God's chastisement and grievous rebuke—that ye shall play your own hearts false; ye shall scatter your sacred tears broadcast upon all waters and string them as precious stones upon each ray of deceitful light; and ye shall pour forth your spirit upon every outlandish slab of marble and let your soul sink into the bosom of every strange stone; and while yet your flesh drips blood among the teeth of them that devour you—ye shall likewise give them the soul of you for food. And for such as hold you abhorred shall ye indeed build Pithom and Raamses—while your children shall be to you for bricks; and when their spirits screech to you from the wood and the stone, their screech will die at the porches of your ears. And he who grows into an eagle among your sons and sprouts him pinions—ye shall cast him from his nest forever; yea, even though he soar in the heights, athirst for the sun and mighty, not for you shall he bring down the luminaries; and should he cleave a cloud with his pinions and make a path for a ray of light, not upon you shall the ray fall; he shall scream upon the tops of the crags far from you and the echo of his voice shall not reach you.

Thus shall ye be bereft of your choicest sons, one by one, and ye shall remain childless. And the glory shall be taken from your habitation and your tent shall be impoverished and shall become a horror and a desolation; the lovingkindness of God shall not pass across the threshold thereof, nor the rejoicing of salvation knock upon the window. And ye shall come to the ruin to pray—and shall not be able; and shall ask for a comforting tear—and there shall be none. The heart is withered and is become as a cluster of squeezed grapes, flung in a corner of the winepress, whereof no drop can be pressed to revive the heart or enliven a ravening soul. And ye shall seek warmth at the stove in the ruin, and its stones shall be cold, and on its chilly ashes a miauling cat And ye shall sit mourning and grieving, the drizzling world without and dust and ashes in the heart. And your eyes shall turn to the deathflies buzzing in your windows and to the spiders in desolate corners, and poverty shall howl at you in the chimney; and the walls of the ruin shall shiver in the cold.

Between the composition of *Surely this People is Grass* and *This too is God's Chas-*

tisement occurred the first Kishineff pogrom (1903). Soon after this pogrom, which shook the Jewish people to its very depths, Bialik wrote his *In the City of Slaughter* (at first, on account of the censorship, entitled *The Burden of Nemirov*).

Bialik describes the horror of the pogroms in lines that move the reader now to impotent rage, now to tears. But that is not the core of this awe-inspiring poem. Its main point is the feebleness and flaccidity, the timorousness and cowardliness of these children of a great race, descendants of the Maccabees and of the martyrs of the Crusades, who, when they had to die, could not even choose a glorious death. The point lies in the contrast between the martyrs of the Crusades, who knew why they were killed just as they knew why they had lived, and these modern victims who " died for no cause as they had lived for none." That faith for which the Jew had once gone to meet death with clear conscience, as lightheartedly as he would go forth to the dance— that faith had ceased to be the chief incentive in the lives of Jews. So it was that, after the pogroms, the one awful cry that should have burst from the heart of the suffering race and terrified this sinful world, full of unpunished murder and violence and the groundless, aimless, endless pains of hell— that cry was never heard:

> And the pain is exceeding great, and exceeding great is the shame. And which of the two is

greater?—say thou, son of man!

In the poet's estimation the shame was the greater; and the shame was the more terrible in that they would fain wash out such awful and unparalleled suffering in tears, and in an unreasoning acquiescence as hateful in the sight of God as the " justifications " of Job's friends, since it arose out of contemptible spiritual feebleness and cowardly hypocrisy:

> And see then, see; they are weltering yet in their grief, they are sunk in their tears, lamenting and mourning. And behold them drumming their hearts and confessing their sins, saying, " We have sinned, have betrayed "—but their hearts do not believe their words . . . Can a broken vessel sin or earthenware fragments transgress? Then why should they entreat Me?—Speak unto them, let them thunder! Let them raise their fists against Me and demand retribution for their shame, the shame of all their generations, first to last; and shiver the Heavens and My seat with their fists . . .

The revolt against Israel's oppressors is here suddenly turned into a revolt against Heaven; and, as often happens when cowardice is self-conscious, the denunciation of cowardice and weakness is turned into its very opposite, and becomes a summons to self-defence and self-reliance.

All Bialik's motifs—the longing for a full life on earth, the craving after love, the revolt against oppression and persecution, the vision of vengeance, the struggle between Judaism and Hellenism in the shape of Aryan civilisation, and the awesome vision of the End—these are all concentrated in his symbolical poem, his profoundest and most sublime work, *The Scroll of Fire*. This is a highly original allegory in which the people of Israel, after losing its natural manner of life as a people living on its own soil in its own country, wanders about in the wilderness of exile, and derives its spiritual nourishment from two strong emotions: hatred for its oppressors and persecutors, and hope of a future redemption. The hatred finds expression in the revenge of the downtrodden, thus described by the " man of angry eyes ":

> Raise me the song of ruin from Abaddon's deeps, black as your heart's embers; bear it amid the nations, scatter it amid the accurst of God, and crush its coals on their head; and sow loss and destruction upon all their meadows, each man round about his four ells. When your shadow passes over the lily of their garden, let it turn black and die; and when your eye meets their marble or their stone image, let it be broken as a shard; and take laughter with you, laughter bitter as wormwood and cruel, wherewith ye shall slay.

All this shall be the revenge for two thousand years of persecutions, oppressions and murders:

> This is the song of fury, fashioned of leaping flame in a night of wrath, from the blood of babe and ancient and the honour of saintly, jewel-like bodies that have been slain.

And the hope of redemption is represented

by the tender "bright-eyed" youth who knows
"the song of consolation and of the hereafter," though he cannot sing this song: for
exile has stifled this song of comfort, has
buried it in the depths of the Jewish heart,
and it cannot be revealed to the world outside
until a new sun rises above the skies of
Judaism, until Judaism emerges from the
Ghetto and comes nearer to the life of this
world. But when this did happen, when
rights began to be given to the Jews, the
earthly and secular life of non-Jewish, Aryan
civilisation at once began to make fierce war
on genuine Judaism. And in this bitter warfare between the heavenly and the earthly,
between the upward striving and the forces
of destruction, it was destruction that had
the victory.

Such is the lamentation sung by the modern
Jeremiah over the destruction of his people.
And like the Jeremiah of history, Bialik, in
the very act of prophesying the final end of
his people, foreshadows a new beginning, the
beginning of a more complete life, in which
not all that is old will be cast out for the sake
of the new, but only that part which has become outworn and has lost its vital value;
and in place of it the new Hebrew life will
absorb into itself all that is best in the
thought and civilisation of our own age.

It is this that Saul TCHERNICHOVSKY
(b. 1875) has felt. He is above all things the
poet of pure art. Not that his muse is a

stranger to reflection or ideas; but his chief concern is with those ancient yet perennially new themes, nature and love. Always he

> Dreams of nightingale-song and laughing light and shadow in the long avenues, and the brook querulous with its hidden voice, and the kisses of burning lips.

As in the Song of Songs, nature and love are interwoven in most of his songs and become a harmonious unity. This is especially apparent in his " Tales of Spring." Here he describes, in lines full of poetic imagery and musical resonance, the effect of the first rays of the spring sun on the flowers that have only just peered up through the soil; on the birds, which have but recently returned from warmer lands; on the insects, which have begun their hurried creeping over the ground; and, last of all, on man. But here the poet breaks away to describe not the effect of nature on man, but the effect of love : in his mind nature and love are linked closely together by an unbreakable bond :

> Life is sunlight and life is love, and where there is no love there is death, the death of the babe without its mother. And in all the world there is no place where there is no sun of love with its rays of light and shaft of grace. But when such a shaft pierces into the inmost heart of man, it brings a witching song out of the deepest treasures of his heart. It is as though the strings of a harp were wakened to song by a skilful hand and tuned to lays of ancient battles fought by a mighty warrior; as though hundreds of fountains

murmuring amid the flower-beds of a garden in the moonlight during a spring month suddenly began to quarrel. The quarrel is a sweet song, with tenderness and pangs in its sweetness, and in the melody are light and spells and heart-beguiling dreams. And the dreams are dreams of light and youth, in which the skies may kiss the earth and the inlets of the sea . . .

After drawing a wonderful picture of the tender, almost indescribable feelings which are stirred in him by these youthful dreams, he continues:

And whoever has once dreamt this dream will be led by it till his dying day; he will pay for it with his heart's blood and his life's sap, it will be graven with a style of adamant upon the tablets of his heart, and only in death will he tear it painfully out of his tender bleeding heart.

The poet himself has seen such a dream:

And I have seen this dream; the spring sun gilded the west, clouds wandered in the sky, and the clouds dripped blood. And the whole land gradually garbed itself in gloom, till it was dim-seeming, with the clouds and the garden . . . And in that hour my heart's desire stood before me, and I was adreaming but my heart was awake, and my eyes saw the maiden and my eyes saw the wreath—a wreath of fireflies about her head like a bright-shining diadem; and the light was tender and hidden, hovering and trembling on the skin. Her eyes were large and dreaming and deeper than the sea, and in them the heavens kissed the secrets of night and the stillness of the sea . . .

Thus are nature and love intertwined in

Tchernichovsky's poems. But this is not the chief or the only thing that distinguishes his love-poems: unlike all other Hebrew poems on the same theme, they show no trace of sentimentalism or plaintiveness, but are full of sap and vigour and the joy of life. The lust of life which he sings is forceful, flaming and unconquerable. It intoxicates, but it likewise exalts; it is healthy, invigorating and exhilarating. There could be no more effective antidote to the Ghetto's two-thousand years of asceticism than the " fiery passion " and the " fiery desire " of which Tchernichovsky sings in his *Tartar Song* (*In the clefts of the Rock*).

Through all his poems runs a strong desire for the complete release of the vital forces which are imprisoned in the shackles of social law and convention. " Not moments of sleep, O Nature, and sweet dreams," he cries in one of his poems, " but passion and warring tempest do I behold in thee." He responds with enthusiasm to everything in nature that is grand and noble. The Prophet Mohammed, who sat calm and unperturbed when the lion's roar cleft the air like thunder, thrills him with awe (*Muhammad*). Bar-Cochba, though he was defeated and killed by Hadrian's superior forces, was none the less a great hero, who brought honour to his people; and only because of his unsuccess and downfall in battle did petty people, who cringe to the victor, dub him " Bar-Coziba " and " false messiah." To the poet he remains still the old "Bar-Cochba," "Son of the Star" (*Before the Sea*). The sight of the ruins of mediæval castles, which have endured through the centuries, stirs in him feelings of reverence towards the ancient lords who once lived in them, those "proud generations," "generations great in faith and mighty in crime"; and he feels a mighty craving for that "forceful fiery will that knows no restraint," that "stormy power" that is revealed in these great structures. He could wish that "his thoughts and deeds might be so expressed," that his every idea might be triumphantly and enduringly carried out, as were the wishes and even the caprices of the "noble generations," "sons of an iron race," who thundered in the walls of their prison—the prison of the tradition and laws of the Mediæval Church—and, breaking through to freedom, raged and stormed like waves when they burst the dam and sweep away in their mighty torrent all that they meet. He could wish to be "blows of a hammer on the anvil of creative effort." More than once he hails the natural elements as "eternal brothers," who in past days long forgotten were divorced from man and no longer recognise in him their brother, no longer know that the roots of the life of man and of silent nature—apparently lifeless, but in truth ever alive and ever young—come from a single source and both have one supreme father (*Musing on*

Things of Old). In one of his most vigorous poems (*Nòcturno*) he turns to nature's enduring elements and begs them to endow him with something at least of their great force and strength:

> Grant me to quench my senses' thirst for life,
> To drain the sea of sorrow to its mire,
> To reel in the flaming tempest of desire,
> Delirious with the dithyrambs of light,
> To gaze on heavenly secrets, glorious might.
> And when life's gale is past, the tumult dead,
> To dare embrace destruction without dread,
> To be through changing aspects, passing hours,
> One thread in the web of universal powers
> That weave in secret or in splendour drest
> Life's riddle that is never to be guessed.

This is indeed to rise up into a higher level of existence, where the secrets of creation and dissolution are revealed, and where man and nature become wholly one.

In his poem *Wood Magic* he describes the "soul-kinship" between man and the denizens of the forest, both the living and the still. "The stones there scattered since the first days of Creation," overgrown with moss, the tiny brook, "the swift rushing stream and the rippling brook that cleave through the vale of mystery," the rabbit's burrow, the mole's tunnel, the ants' nest and the "families" of mushrooms—all alike are dear to him, and to them all he offers the same greeting: "Life and strength to you! Blessed be ye all both petty and great!"—though in truth there is nothing in nature that is petty: all is great and worthy; each is an inseparable part of the great " All " of divine nature. The poet grieves that he cannot understand the speech of the beasts and birds, the speech of the palm trees and the grass. But

> Surely there is one who understands the chatter of waves, the whispering of the branches; who grieves with the grape when its skin reddens late; who kisses the pine-trunk with manifold mercy when it leans before breaking. And to whom does the oak nod its head? And with whom does the wind converse as it passes?
>
> There is one who holds sweet converse at night with the bashful mushrooms, who comes to play with the water-spiders riding on the bubbles; who rejoices over the nest of a black thrush, and is glad at the happiness of the mother-bird, and hisses to the nimble lizard " take heed! There's a foe in the stubble! "
>
> There must be one who mourns barefoot and rends his garments for the field that is bared by the axe and given over to the workshop.

Such is Tchernichovsky's attitude to nature. The enduring things of the world, field, forest, pool, lizard, thrush and mushroom, are all of them his brothers, his own flesh and bone, his brothers in nature and the life-force, his brothers in the divinity that embraces all things and to all things gives life. They all have a single root, a single basis of their being, a single source of life. This is the *hen kai pan* which was the cornerstone of the philosophy of the great Greek thinkers, and which was so remote from the conception of the Jewish Prophets and Sages, in whose eyes all nature was in the hands of the one and only God " as clay in the hands of the potter."

Tchernichovsky the Jew is far more akin to the Greek philosophers than to the Sages of his own people. To the question, "Who and where is his God?" he answers (*Visions of the False Prophets*):

> He is here on earth too and the heavens are not His—and He has given the earth to Man.
>
> A handsome tree, a pleasant mead—His likeness is likewise in them, and He conceals Himself on every lofty hill; wherever is the sense of life and flesh and blood, in growing plant and silent mineral He takes shape.
>
> And His family is—whatsoever exists: the hind and the tortoise, the plant and the cloud big with thunder; for no God of spirits is He: God is the Heart; that is His Name and His memorial forever.

His strong affection for ancient Greece, the land of Homer and Anacreon (both of whose works he has translated), is shown in a number of poems written in the spirit of Nietzche's philosophy. This is how he describes the ideal Greece in his *Deianira*:

> A land by blue seas hearkening to happy waves, a land of rounded hills, their brows crowned with olive and pine, like smaragdus stone in a golden setting, gold and scarlet fabrics where wheat and oats are planted. A land wherein the streams and springs flow from hidden places in the marble, the rock-caverns being their sources; purer are they than the tears of the well-nymphs. The dreaming

skies appear like wide-open blue eyes; myrtle groves and laurel trees—the realm of holy quiet, veiled in hidden secrets and wonders; and in their shade are marble fanes like a poet's dreams embodied and set stock-still in stone. And in this land of wonders wander graceful goddesses, eternal in their beauty, blossoming as in the spring of the world, coveting and loving life in the storms and pleasures of desire, awe-inspiring loveliness of marble in their faces, but their hearts a flaming fire. With them are giant gods, bearing dominion and dread, mighty and virile, and their muscles of steel; near to Man and his heart, and desirous of his happiness and joy. And the men of that land are joyous and beautiful, and there is strength in their loins, and in them wisdom and might embrace, and they too are like gods. A generation that knows the lusts of its soul and is not ashamed of the storms of its desire, but will rise to consuming love, and valorously take vengeance on its foes.

Such is Tchernichovsky's Hellenic ideal. It is so very far from the ideal of Judaism, that a clash between the two was inevitable. The Jewish poet even bows *Before the Image of Apollo*, and chants a hymn of praise to the young and joyous Greek god of culture —the god of the heroic age which still beheld gods on earth and still drank its fill from life's cup. This god is utterly foreign to the Jewish people, sickly in body and broken in spirit—" the house of sufferers " as the poet contemptuously calls it. And the Jewish poet turns to the Greek Apollo :

I come to thee—dost thou know me? I am the Jew, and there is eternal strife between us.

All the oceans that divide continent from continent, with their multitudinous raging waters, could not fill to the brim the abyss that lies between us. The skies and sandy wastes are too short to span the breach between the *Torah* of my fathers and the faith of those who hold thee in honour.

The Jewish poet bows the knee to the image of the Greek Apollo because he revolts against the age-long death-agony of Judaism, and his soul has already snapped the spiritual fetters and come close to a healthy mundane life. " The race has grown senile : its god has grown senile too ! " So the poet cries with a daring such as never before found expression in Hebrew. But the time has come for the ancient people's resurrection, and both the people and its god will return to the days of their youth, to the days of the Judges and the Song of Songs.

Feelings that were choked by the hands of those who are gone have revived from the prison of untold generations. " God's light! God's light! " every bone cries within me, " Life! Only Life! " each sinew and muscle, "Divine Light and Life!"

And so I come to thee. I come to thee, bow to thine image, the symbol of the light that is in life; I bow and kneel to the good and exalted, to all that is loftiest in the whole Universe, to all that is glorious in Creation, to all that is highest in the innermost secrets of the Maker. I kneel to Life, to valour and beauty, I kneel to all loveliness which corpse-like men, the corrupt seed of Adam, rebelling against life, have robbed from the hand of my rock the Almighty, the supreme God of the awesome desert, supreme God of those who subdued Canaan as a whirlwind—and then bound him with phylacteries.

This Jewish Hellenist's Apollo is in fact the God of Israel; not, however, the God of the Talmudic era and the preceding centuries, but the God who is both " the Ancient of Days " and yet ever young, the God of Israel in the days of the Judges, *El-Shaddai*, the " Vigorous God," a God who loves force and strength no less than did Apollo. He who ordained " Not a soul shall be kept alive!" when this was a vital need—he it is that speaks through the lips of the false prophets, whom Tchernichovsky restores to their former repute (*Visions of the False Prophets*)—those prophets for whom country and state were more precious than abstract spirituality and lofty ethics. It was only after the " moralists " had gained the victory, and the kingdom of Israel had perished, and the long and gloomy life of exile began, that it became possible to call by the name of " bandits " and " ruffians " those Zealots of Roman times, the great warriors who fought to deliver the second Jewish State from the Roman yoke. Their strength and courage, their thirst for a free national life, were reckoned to their blame and not to their credit. And when the exiles from Jerusalem are asked (*Songs of Exiles*) "What befell the tombs of the Zealots, those heroes afire for freedom?" the ironical answer is:

> Ask the kite of the hills that picked their eyes, ask the dog where he cracks his bones, ask the wind where it scatters its dust—but do not ask your people, its leaders and its wise men, who call the best of its sons "lawless men", and blot the names of its true saints out of its heart and its books . . .

So Tchernichovsky reproves his people. Like Bialik, he too condemns their weakness and surrender. Yet when we read his great historical poem *Baruch of Mayence* (which, although it deals with an historical subject and was written a year and a half before the Kishineff pogrom, offers a kind of parallel to Bialik's *In the City of Slaughter*), we see again that between these two poets there lies a gulf as wide and deep as between the God of Israel and the Greek Apollo.

The scene is laid in Catholic Mayence in the 11th or 12th century. The mob has attacked the Jews, and there has been an orgy of fire and rapine, maiming and murder. The only salvation for the Jews lies in abjuring their faith. A few of them resolve to adopt this course. The wife of Baruch of Mayence has been killed by the mob, and Baruch kills his two daughters with his own hand:

> This the first sacrifice have I offered since we were exiled and our Temple destroyed

says Baruch, and he thus explains his horrible cruelty:

> For alas! I could no longer bear my bitter fate: to let my daughters fall into the hands of the foe,

into the hands of a people that ever lusts only for blood; so that my daughters 'neath the foe's roof should forget all that is holy and precious to me, all that for which I have given rivers of blood, and that their offspring should go with the merry, boisterous throng, clad in silken fabrics, to see Jews burning at the stake.

But after this awful effort of will Baruch's mind becomes unhinged, and when the rioters bid him deny his faith, in his confusion and disorder of mind he mumbles assent. Forthwith rude hands seize him and drag him to the church. There he sees dumb images, which yet seem to speak to him and say:

> Stone are we, and have no heart—that is our strength and our greatness: the whole world prostrates itself before our feet of stone. Our footsteps shake all creation and set the earth a-tremble. Kneel thou likewise, worm! For thy gods are we!

He kneels and prostrates himself; but this prostration, done under compulsion, provokes in him the bitterest hatred for his cruel enemies, and from his heart burst frightful curses, the like of which would be sought in vain in Hebrew literature. He sits imprisoned in the monastery, meditating vengeance the whole day long. He ponders means of wreaking vengeance on his people's foes, his wife's murderers, who have made him his daughters' murderer. Late in the night he sets fire to the monastery. The fire spreads all through the city, and he himself, now driven out of his mind, hastens to his wife's newly-dug grave, and tells his dead wife the story of the revenge that he has taken on their enemies, gloating in his incipient madness over the great conflagration which his terrible vengeance has kindled.

What a difference between this attitude towards the pogroms and that of Bialik! Here, in Tchernichovsky's poem, all the deadly hatred, stored up through centuries against the oppressors and persecutors of the Jews, bursts out in violent curses and threats, and reveals itself in feelings of savage vengeance; whereas in Bialik's *Burden of Nemirov* the indignation aroused by the weakness of the Jews finds its outlet in cries of despair and bitter complaints against the Jews themselves —though the complaints are like strokes of the hammer on the anvil.

This difference is not accidental. Bialik has a deep reverence for Judaism though he castigates the Jews. Tchernichovsky is at times as hostile as Nietzsche towards Judaism, but regards the Jews as a healthy and vigorous people. This is evident in his beautiful idylls, in which, as in his narrative poems, he shows a truly epic quality. These idylls do not set out to prove anything, and the narrative element in them is very slight; but in spite of the absence of deliberate purpose we derive from them a new conception of the middle classes of present-day Jewry, especially in the Crimea, where Tchernichovsky was born, and in Southern

Russia, where he spent his youth. These Jews observe the Jewish religion and respect Jewish customs, yet without any rigid orthodoxy or austerity. They are in close contact with their non-Jewish neighbours, and are not only influenced by them, but influence them in turn. They are active and practical and find zest in life. To them Jewish customs do not mean asceticism and self-denial: Sabbaths, holy-days, circumcisions, betrothals and marriages and all the joyous religious ceremonies bring cheerfulness and light into their lives, together with purely mundane pleasures. These pleasures and simple Jewish celebrations are described by Tchernichovsky in a series of extremely beautiful idylls, such as *The Close of the Sabbath*, *Hakkafoth** and especially *The Circumcision*, an idyll which, for the breadth of its canvas, its artistic perfection and its " epic " calm, deserves to be ranked with Goethe's *Hermann and Dorothea*. Among other gems are the idylls *The Pancackes*, *The Sick Berele* and *The Heat of the Day*. In Hebrew literature only Mendelé Mocher Sefarim has reached such a high level of objective portrayal of life and artistic colouring. But Mendelé, whose influence is very apparent in these idylls, described only the life of the poorer people, and his brush never had the same breadth as that of the Jewish Hellenist Saul Tchernichovsky.

*A procession in the Synagogue on the festival of the " Rejoicing in the Law."

What is the ideal of this Hebrew poet with the Greek spirit? In his poem *I believe* he says:

> I believe in the future too: though the day be yet far distant, come it will, when nation from nation shall receive peace and benediction. Then my people also will blossom once more, and a generation will arise in the Land which, freed from iron chains, will gaze on the light with steadfast eyes, and live and love and work and fashion: a generation living in very truth on the land, not in a heavenly future, nor content with spiritual life. In that day a poet, with heart awake to all that is beautiful and noble, will sing a new song; and for that youthful poet's garland they will pluck flowers from my grave.

Such is the ideal of the poet of the Hebrew revival. He finds no satisfaction in spirituality alone: he is not " content with spiritual life." With the Prophets, he hopes that in the future hatred among nations will disappear, and that truth and peace will prevail between nation and nation; but in his poems the " truth " and " peace " of the Prophets go hand in hand with " beauty " and " worldly life."

Two more recent poets, Jacob COHEN (b. 1880) and Z. SHNEUR (b. 1887), have gone beyond even Tchernichovsky. They no longer champion Greek ideals against Jewish morality. They take modern life and its worldly culture for granted; and if they criticise, it is as poets and as human beings, not specifically as Jews. With Tchernichovsky the object is still to take worldly life, love and nature and graft them by force on to Judaism; Jacob Cohen accepts them as his due, as the gift of heaven to the elect of mankind, of no matter what nation. Jacob Cohen is a typical " romantic." There is in his love-poems a peculiar tenderness and an appealing simplicity. When he describes nature without attempting to be " powerful " and rebellious, his language is rich and musical, delicate and soft. Such poems as *I know a Damsel, Beautiful and Tender, Queen of the Morning, Hidden Melodies, The Laughing Generation* and *Sunset* have a lily-like fragrance. But his poetic power fails him when he would " rise up in rebellion " and " erupt." He, too, like Tchernichovsky, sings of the Zealots (in his *Ruffians*); but while Tchernichovsky's poems are full of force and vigour, short and swift and unerring in aim, Jacob Cohen's poems are marred by affectation and rhetoric. His muse is at its best in depicting the quiet charm of nature and the delicate sweetness of love; it is powerless to stir up a storm or provoke the combative instincts in his reader. On the other hand, his poetical style, so long as it ranges over those topics which are within his scope, almost reaches the pitch of perfection : it is highly finished and polished and is perfectly suited to its subject.

Shneur possesses what Cohen lacks. His poetry is remarkably forceful and vigorous, and his speculation ranges over wide horizons. He is original and resourceful in his choice of subjects and in his metaphors. Nothing daunts him. If Bialik is the poet of the country town, and Tchernichovsky the poet of the village, Shneur is the best of the city. While Bialik's affection is for the Jewish past, and Tchernichovsky's longing is for the Jewish future, Shneur is the embodiment of the Jewish present. Shneur, like Bialik and Tchernichovsky, rebels against God; but whereas they rebel only against the God of Israel, and do indeed rebel, Shneur rebels also against the God of the world, and, if the truth be told, does not so much rebel as blaspheme with concentrated fury.

In his poem *The Strains of the Mandoline* he seeks the cause of the destruction of beauty on earth, and finds it in religion. In *It shall come to pass in the Latter Days* he does not shrink from attacking the highest prophetic ideal—the most exalted form of the Messianic hope, in the sense of its noble aspiration for world peace and complete and absolute equality. But he can do more than attack Judaism. In his *Songs of Israel* (part of *The Strains of the Mandoline*) he exposes the vileness of the great world, which has drained Jewry dry, has robbed it of its choicest belongings and falsified all its documents, and now considers itself noble and Jewry a base slave. The poet sees Israel withdrawing farther and farther from its own land, the land of the sun, into cold countries, and he summons his people to return " to the sun," to its sun-scorched homeland. In his great lyric poem *In the Mountains* he deplores the fact that the Ghetto child is a stranger to the free healthy air of the mountains. This poem is, however, in the main filled with legends and descriptions and philosophico-poetical ideas, entirely unconnected with Jews and Judaism. These descriptions and ideas place Shneur on the level of the greatest European poets. Restraint, simplicity and tenderness are qualities not found in Shneur's work; in all these he falls behind Bialik, Tchernichovsky and Cohen; but, on the other hand, he has a breadth of conception, a loftiness of vision and courage of expression never before attained by even the greatest of Hebrew poets.

Shneur, too, like Tchernichovsky, sings of "the fire of desire." But while in Tchernichovsky the longing is kissed by sunshine, and full of light and sweetness, with Shneur the longing is insatiable, a thing of terror and mystery. Hence Shneur is always harping on death, night and gloom. He sees the entire world wrapped in a murky fog:

> And in the troubled mist struggle men, cold without and cold within. For their spirits are also ice and their hearts a cold shapeless lump; they run to seek fire, to seek a God to warm body and soul; yet will not find ere they perish.

In another poem (*Ma'aseh*) he writes:

Life and death are two demons who have made a pact to play with dwarfs. " I will fashion creatures and thou shalt slay them, and we will make a sport of quick and dead . . ." The one creates writhing mannikins and flings them into the rushing, plangent spate of Time; the other takes them and stamps on them, and the spate bears away their carcasses to a dark Infinity.

After such ideas it is not surprising that in the work of this fearless poet chill grief penetrates even through the mask of an unbridled effrontery, and even through the exhilaration of drunkenness. This is illustrated in his great poem *The Vision of Desolation*. Fame, love, poetry, all the pleasures of city life—all end in desolation with its bald skull and empty eye-sockets. The young poet draws aside too far the curtain behind which lurk death and dissolution and ultimate nothingness.

Among the younger writers there are several others of established reputation. David SHIMONOVITZ (b. 1886) is a gifted poet, and one of the few Hebrew writers with a thorough knowledge of Palestine. He has painted the charm of the country in his poems (*The Jordanite*) and stories (*The Wanderer Out of Time* and *A Vineyard by Night*). He deals also with profound subjects of speculation, and seeks after new forms of creative expression. Jacob FICHMANN (b. 1881), poet and critic, is more individualistic than any other of the modern Hebrew poets; his is a wonderfully sad and tender muse, and a lucid and beautiful style, but his palette is not rich in colours, and his poems lack vigour and force and a due measure of light and shade. As a critic he shows a fine appreciation of the sublime and great intellectual acumen. Jacob STEINBERG (b. 1886) is original in his ideas and methods of presentation, but he has not yet developed along a line of his own. Isaac KATZENELSOHN (b. 1886) is the poet of the gladness of life, and in his light and dainty songs all is music and melody.

Elhanan Löb LEVINSKY (1853-1910) occupies a unique position as a feuilletonist of genius. He was more than a writer of pleasing *causeries* suited to the daily Press. There is not a single problem of Jewish life that is left untouched in the fifty chapters of his miscellanies contributed under the general title *Thoughts and Deeds* to the first twenty-three volumes of *Ha-Shiloah*. Levinsky was not only a first-rate journalist, but a real philosopher. His is the optimistic and cheerful philosophy that has its roots in a staunch belief in the goodness inherent in mankind and in the world, and rests on a true understanding of life. A feuilletonist of this type could not fail to give rein to his imagination; and in 1891 Levinsky wrote *A Journey to Palestine in the year* 2040 (Odessa, 1893), in which he presents a stirring picture of the new Jewish life in a revived Palestine, a free and healthy life of honest toil, rich in spiritual content.

Among recent novelists mention should be made of the short-lived J. BERSHADSKY (Dumashevisky, 1870-1908). In his two long novels *Without a Goal* (1899), and *Against the Stream* (1901), and in his many short stories, he depicts a new type—the petty Jewish bourgeoisie and the intellectual proletariat which have risen on the ruins of the old patriarchal régime. In his first novel Bershadsky shows, in the character of Adamovitz " a man who lacks God "—a man without ideal or faith or principles, who is all greed and selfishness; and his greed and selfishness are not of the kind that leads to action, but are purely negative and destructive. Introspection and self-analysis annihilate in the intelligent and highly gifted Adamovitz that simplicity and directness of feeling which alone makes it possible to enjoy life and to be a useful member of a society or a nation. Lacking any belief or principle, a mere human being of Jewish stock, with no sort of restraint, Adamovitz has the " courage " to follow his instincts and do whatever his heart desires; he goes to the length of seducing a girl who has trusted him. But his hypercritical temperament robs his " courage " of its reward, and he remains crumbled and crushed and neither one thing nor the other, without high aspirations and without even half securing the object of his lust. In his second novel Bershadsky attempts a sketch of an orthodox *Maskil* of the type of Pines and Jawitz, who wishes to swim " against the stream "—to educate his sons in a religious-nationalist spirit, inclining rather to orthodoxy, to the "Mizrachi" school of Zionism. But his sons slip away from him one by one, and even his plan of establishing himself in Palestine comes to grief on the rock of circumstances, so that he remains frustrated on both sides.

Bershadsky was a realist. He was influenced by the realistic tendency in Russian literature, from which he acquired not so much an objective outlook on life as a capacity for describing its outward forms. But he was also a psychologist: he knew and could describe the soul-ferment that went on in all his heroes—more indeed in the manner of a psychopathist than of a creative artist. There is in his stories very little imagination, descriptive power, or real creativeness. He photographed rather than painted, and tended to put thoughts and ideas into the mouths of his heroes instead of allowing them the ideas and thoughts which would have been naturally theirs as a result of their characters and activities. His style matches his subject-matter: it is highly matter-of-fact and accurate, but it lacks imaginativeness and is poor in the softer shades.

What Bershadsky lacked is found abundantly in S. BEN-ZION (S. Guttmann, b. 1870). His stories are full of softness and tenderness, and are particularly remarkable for the beauty of their rich and delicate language. He can describe the soul of the child with its great little joys and sorrows. In his long story, *A Broken Soul* (1902), he portrays in clear colours the tyranny of the orthodox Jewish family of the past generation, which, with its many demands on the child and the numerous prohibitions imposed on his tender soul, kills him spiritually, and raises up a generation of miserable " external students," ne'er-do-wells, with ailing bodies and feeble, crushed and featureless souls. These types Ben-Zion has depicted with great art in his other long story, *Beyond Life* (1904). In one of his short stories, *The Temptation of Spring*, he describes the joy and happiness of a boy set free from the bondage of the *Heder* before the feast of Passover—the festival of Spring and freedom. The beautiful and emotional lines out of the Song of Songs, which have remained in the boy's memory as the result of repetition in the *Heder*, come back to him, and in his mind become one with the revival and renascence of nature, until they are intermingled in one glorious, sweet song.

But Ben-Zion has written not only of child-life. In the story *Meshi* ("Silk"), he describes a young and idealistic nationalist, who wastes away among the narrow-minded and unenterprising bourgeoisie of an out-of-the-way town. The idyll *Old People*, in which he reaches his highest artistic level, combines simplicity and warm sympathy; and in his sketches, *A Long Letter* and *Souvenirs*, he describes the effect of the pogroms on the more idealistic and sensitive Jews, and how they are harrowed by the profanation of what their people hold sacred. In general, all Ben-Zion's work betrays a deep love for historic Judaism and Jewish spiritual values; yet there is for the most part no tendency to condone their bad side, and no emotional exaggeration.

Joseph Hayyim BRENNER (1881-1921) and G. SHOFMANN (b. 1880) are almost the antithesis the one of the other. Brenner's novels deal with social problems, Shofmann's with individual problems.

Brenner sees Jewish life, in all its branches and social strata, as a great sink of evil. In his long novels, *In Winter* (1903) and *Round About the Point* (1904), in his profound drama *Beyond the Frontiers* (1907), and in his numerous short stories, he depicts the hopelessly wretched life of a people lacking an independent territorial or spiritual foundation—a life that is but one long series of anomalies and of purposeless and endless pain and suffering. The poverty and gloom of the "Jewish quarter," especially among the poorer classes, drive Brenner to a pitch of grief and despondency that fill him with gloomy desperation : he can see no goal or end and no way out.

In no less degree is he revolted by the semi-educated class of Jews. Those who have been brought up on the study of the Talmud in *Heder* and *Yeshivah* have crammed their young minds with the old scholastic casuistry, and so are bereft of any sense of actuality; while the radicals and socialists " of Jewish origin," who have no interest in anything Jewish, have also crammed their minds with academic casuistries, the only difference being that their abstractions are utterly foreign to Jewry, since they have been imported from without and have no basis in Jewish national life. Both alike live in a world that is wholly abstract and unreal. Both alike have exchanged real full-blooded life for barren theories; but the socialists and radicals have gone further, in that they have substituted for the home-made Jewish casuistry some foreign catchword or interest to which they cannot possibly feel any inner spiritual affinity. Marxian theories of life have fostered casuistry and scholasticism among socialists of this type (*In Winter*). As for Zionism, its advocates, from force of habit, have reduced it to empty verbiage and vulgarised it. The great idea of revival has become for them merely a subject for pointless and rhetorical speeches and harangues. This "mouldy corpse" is incapable of achieving any concrete national purpose; it is not even capable of any " spiritual exaltation " worth the name (*Round About the Point*).

Nay more: into Palestine itself, and into the two most important national objects—the colonising of the ancient home-land and the spread of a new Hebrew culture—there has been introduced the same " Galuth " spirit, which finds ample room for speechifying and bargaining, but no room for real creative labour. Brenner, who spent the last years of his life in Palestine, gave expression to these latter views in his novels *Between Sea and Sea* (1910), *From Here and There* (1911) and *Bereavement and Frustration* (1920).

In the west-European Ghetto he sees the self-same conditions, and perhaps even worse. While there are in his Palestinian stories many bright spots and many idealistic characters, his *Beyond the Frontiers*, a drama with a profound central idea, describing Jewish Ghetto life in London, is replete with awful and blood-curdling incidents. Brenner's pessimism goes very deep. He certainly makes the bad appear worse than it is by the mere fact of ignoring the good. Yet the bad which he describes does for the most part exist; and Brenner, oblivious of the fact that " evil is but a throne for what is good," cried to heaven by reason of the violence of his suffering. He turned publicist, critic, and party-organiser, but nowhere found rest for his aching spirit. He was murdered near Jaffa in the disturbances of May, 1921.

G. Shofmann is a new kind of novelist in Hebrew literature. Life does not move him to deep feeling or a cry of pain : he merely describes. He portrays not social but individual types. He describes the Jewish " decadent " in the widest sense of the term. His characters are original and reflective types, who feel and suffer deeply; but they are superfluous, failures alike in society and in affairs. They are lonely, isolated beings, tormented in body and mind, " outsiders " whose lives are made up of introspection and hypercriticism. They are, however, *Jewish* solitaries, whose isolation, superfluity and uselessness are the result partly of their Jewish upbringing, and partly of the abnormal condition of the Jewish people in exile. Shofmann sometimes portrays healthy types, as, for example, in his attractive sketches *Love* and *The Vengeance of a Barrel-Organ*; but here also he is entirely objective and self-controlled, economical in his use of words, and hitting the mark with every word. His art is very much that of the sculptor. He is the true artist, who knows the secret of brevity.

E. N. GENESIN (1880-1913) was a writer of exceptional gifts. He was one of those wandering souls and earnest seekers whose life is a puzzle and whose work is an enigma. Throughout his brief and unhappy career he depicted only the dark corners of life; his subjects are dumb souls, sunk within themselves, suffering endlessly and uncomplainingly. Genesin loved the shadows and half-lights in nature and the human soul, and he portrayed them in his handful of sketches. These are unique in Hebrew literature alike for their methods of description and for their obscure style, which is admirably suited to their vague subject-matter. Genesin is the most individual and aloof of Hebrew story-writers.

Among other recent Hebrew novelists mention should be made of " Kh'wajah Musa " (Moses SMILANSKY, b. 1874), who has ably depicted Arab life in a series of sketches entitled *Sons of Arabia*, and A. A. KABAK (b. 1882), who, in his novels *Alone* (1905), *Daniel Shafranov* (1911) and *Victory* (1923), has described the relations between the Zionist movement and the Russian emancipation movement, and in his three-volume historical novel, *Shelomoh Molko* (London, 1927-1929), has drawn an interesting historical sketch of the life of the Marranos or Pseudo-Jews in Spain and of the Cabbalists in Safad.

S. J. AGNON (b. 1888) has specialised in descriptions of Hasidic life in Galicia fifty years ago. He is among the most gifted artists in Hebrew literature to-day.

J. D. BERKOVITZ (b. 1885) describes with delicate humour the life of the Lithuanian Jew. His chief merit, however, lies in his Hebrew translation of the Yiddish writings of Shalom Aleichem, an artistic achievement whereby the works of that great humorist have been retrieved for Hebrew literature.

M. Secco (Meir Smelansky, b. 1876) well describes the settled, spacious, happy life of the Jews of the Ukraine before the pogroms of 1919-1921, as well as the actual horrors of those pogroms.

H. Hasas has portrayed the upheaval brought about in Jewish life through the Russian revolution and the World War. His great powers of observation enable him to reproduce the most delicate nuances in the feelings of the modern Jew, who, though forcibly torn away from Judaism, still retains enough of it to keep him from becoming an ordinary human type.

Asher Barash is a craftsman of high merit. His sketches illustrate the extraordinary materialism and worldliness of the Hasidic mystics of Galicia. Barash describes this life with a wealth of detail, and welds its worldly and spiritual elements into a unique and harmonious whole.

J. Burla has described the life of the Sephardi Jews in novels notable for their highly imaginative character and originality of conception. He has been the first to paint a picture of these Jews, who have inhabited Palestine since the expulsion from Spain and even earlier.

A. Steinmann deals with the tragedy of a particular type of modern Jew, doomed to restless discontent, first by the lack of a regular and systematic upbringing, then by the conflicting influence of city life and the insis-

tent cravings of an individualistic and self-centred existence that lacks both a land beneath it and a new God above it.
AVIGDOR MEIRI (Feuerstein) re-tells, both as novelist and as poet, the horrors of the War. In his poems he laments the shortcomings of Jewry in its present transition from exile to freedom, from Europe to the Land of Israel. U. Z. GRUNBERG also denounces these shortcomings in poems which at times re-echo the early Prophets, but suffer from a defective technique.
Less profound but more artistic is A. SHLIONSKY, the youngest and most modern of the living Hebrew poets who have made their mark.
Mention may be made of two living scholars who have played an important part in Hebrew literature. SIMON BERNFELD (b. 1860) has dealt in popular form with a very wide range of subjects in various fields of learning and literature. J. KLATZKIN is a gifted writer of philosophical essays, whose radical outlook on life may be classed as the absolute antithesis of " Spiritual Zionism." In place of the religious and moral abstract values of Ahad Ha-Am, Klatzkin sets up as the centre of his scheme two single values—the Land and the Language.
Within the last ten years Hebrew literature has been enriched by a wealth of works on Jewish and general learning, both original and translated, as well as by numerous trans-

lations of novels, particularly from English and German. It is well on the way to becoming a complete national literature, which takes all human concerns as its province. Bearing in mind that modern Hebrew literature is but the latest link in a literary chain that stretches back through at least three thousand years, and that it has absorbed into itself the essence of human thought from the days of Egypt and Babylon, Greece and Rome, Spain and Italy, to the present day, we cannot but recognise its enormous potentialities, and may predict for it an illustrious future on that historic soil whereon it was born thousands of years ago, and whereon it has now returned to life.

GLOSSARY
OF UNTRANSLATED TERMS

1. BATLAN (lit. one not occupied in worldly business). From the earliest times a Jewish congregation used to maintain ten or more men who were at leisure to fulfil the community's religious requirements, such as attendance at the daily synagogue services, for which a minimum of ten men is necessary, and a multiplicity of other religious and quasi-religious duties. The name for these, " Batlan," pl. " Batlanim," is as early as the Mishnah. In the last century the word has become a term of depreciation, signifying the type of Jew who lacks ability in the more practical affairs of life.

2. BETH HA-MIDRASH (lit. " House of Study "). A building, either the Synagogue itself or a room adjoining it, devoted to the study of the Law and to prayers, and to Jewish communal purposes. It is the most characteristic institution of orthodox Jewish life, the centre of religious and public interests and a sort of " club-house " for the community.

3. CABBALAH (lit. tradition). The esoteric, mystical manner of interpreting the Pentateuch, which embodies a theosophic conception of life. It became popular among

Jews from early mediæval times, but is supposed to continue the Gnostic strain of earlier centuries.

4. GALUTH (lit. "exile"). The Jewish dispersion; the condition of Jews living in exile away from Palestine; used in a depreciatory sense of the material and mental condition supposed to affect Jews who have lost all sense of national patriotism.

5. GEMARA (lit. completion). The TALMUD consists of text (known as Mishnah) and commentary, which is called Gemara. See also Mishnah.

6. HASIDIM (pl. of Hasid, lit. "pious," "saintly"). In the 18th century in Eastern and Central Europe, as a reaction against the dry formalism then characteristic of the Jewish religious life, a popular and widespread movement arose which, while cultivating the mystical "cabbalistic" aspect of Judaism, gave to it a more popular tinge. As opposed to the emphasis which was placed on diligent study of the Talmud and its commentaries, it emphasised the emotional elements in religion. At first it aroused intense opposition from the representatives of the older and more conventional orthodoxy, but it gradually came to terms with its "opponents" (*mithnagg'dim*) and has persisted as a standard variation within Jewish orthodoxy. Its leaders, TZADDIKIM (pl. of Tzaddik, lit. "righteous one"), or Rebbiim (pl. of Rebbe—a conventional pro-

nunciation of Rabbi, "master," "teacher"), are the objects of popular veneration; they are credited with miraculous powers, and, owing to their exceptional piety, are believed to have intimate communion with the Deity. Hasidism tended to many of the cruder forms of religious superstition, and provided the main target for the more aggressive of the "enlightened" Jews of the later HASKALAH period.

7. HASKALAH (lit. "rationalism," the cultivation of "sekhel," the reason). It stands for the German "Aufklärung," and in English it is usually rendered by "enlightenment" or "intellectual renaissance." It is the antithesis of uncritical acceptance of tradition. Its advocates are called MASKILIM (pl. of Maskil, a word occurring in the Old Testament in the sense of "wise" or "prudent"). Haskalah among the Jews of the late 18th and early 19th centuries took the form of popularising subjects of secular learning and resisting the restrictions of Jewish orthodoxy.

8. HEDER (lit. "small chamber"), the name given to the old traditional system of elementary education among the Jews. The sole subject of study was the Hebrew Pentateuch with the mediæval commentary of Rashi, and parts of the Talmud. Children were sent to such schools at a very early age.

9. MASKILIM. See HASKALAH.

10. MELITZAH (lit. "figurative language."

Cf. Prov. I, 6, "figure," RV. mg. "interpretation"): the name applied to the artificial metaphorical style cultivated in certain phases of mediæval and modern Hebrew literature. It is the exact counterpart of "euphuism," the literary style made popular for a time in English literature by Lyly's "Euphues" (end of 16th century). Its characteristics are "affected artificiality of style, indulgence in antithesis and simile and conceits, subtly refined choice of words, preciosity" (Fowler, "Modern English Usage").

11. MISHNAH (lit. "teaching by means of repetition"). The collection of Jewish oral tradition, supplementing and interpreting and, so far as later needs required, adapting the body of legislation contained in the Pentateuch. It was compiled, mainly on the basis of earlier rabbinical authorities, by Rabbi Judah the Patriarch at Sepphoris in Galilee at the close of the 2nd century C.E. It forms the basis of the discussions which make up the two Talmuds—the Jerusalem (or Palestinian) Talmud and the Babylonian Talmud—which were completed at the close of the 4th and 5th centuries respectively.

12. REBBIS. See Hasidim.

13. SHULHAN ARUKH (lit. "A table set in array"). A corpus of laws dealing with every detail of the life of a Jew who would live in conformity with the religious

standards enjoined in the Bible and the Talmud. It was compiled by Joseph Caro (1488-1575) at Safad in Palestine. It soon became, and still is, the authoritative code of Rabbinical Judaism.

14. TALMUD (lit. " study, learning "). See GEMARA and MISHNAH.

15. TANNAIM (lit. " teachers "). The early Jewish authorities of the first two centuries C.E., whose sayings and teachings are recorded in the Mishnah (and contemporary literature). They are the direct successors to the Pharisees, who in turn succeeded the " Elders " and " Soferim " (scribes) as the repositories of the Oral Law, which supplemented the Written Law of the Pentateuch.

16. TZADDIK. See HASIDIM.

17. YESHIVAH (lit. " sitting, session "). The Jewish " College " or " Upper School," in which the old traditional system of purely religious education was continued beyond the stage of the HEDER. Instruction was confined to the study of Mishnah, Talmud and Talmudic commentaries.

18. YIDDISH (" Jüdisch," Jewish). The name given to the related German jargons spoken by the Jews of Eastern and Central Europe (who took the language with them when they emigrated to America and England). It is a dialect of Middle-High-German with a considerable admixture of Hebrew words, and is written in Hebrew characters

INDEX

"Abgad ha-Edrei," 137.
Abiezer, 26.
Abramovitz (Shalom Jacob), (See "Mendelé Mocher Sefarim").
"Adam Hakohen" (Dov Hakohen Lebensohn), 21, 28—32, 45.
Against the Stream, 184.
Agnon (S. J.), 191.
"Ahad Ha-Am" (Asher Ginzberg), 120-128, 136, 138, 144, 146, 193.
Ahavath Tziyon, 45-49, 51, 52, 53.
"Ahiasaf" publishing company, 138.
Ahijah the Shilonite, 25.
Ait Tzavu'a, 53ff., 61.
Alone (Bialik), 153.
Alone (Kabak), 191.
Amulet, The, 143.
Asenath, daughter of Potiphera, 65, 68.
Asaka D'rispak, 73.
Asif, ha-, 109.
Ashmath Shomeron, 50.
Assembly of Sages, 63.
At Evening, 143.
Athaliah's Requital, 8.
At the Parting of the Ways, 122.
Austria, Jews of, 6, 8.
Avigdor Meiri (Feuerstein), 193.
Barash (Asher), 192.
"Bar Cocheba," 166f.
" Bar-Derora," 63.
Barkai, 111.
Baruch of Mayence, 174-6.
Batlan (See Gloss. 1).
Before the Image of Apollo, 171f.
Before the Sea, 167.
Ben Abuyah, 14.
"Ben Avigdor," 134-6.
"Ben-Netz" (W. Winchefsky), 63.
Ben Yehuda (Eliezer), 99, 102-4, 137.
Ben Zev (Judah Löb), 5.
Ben Zion (S.), (S. Guttmann), 185-7.
Berdichevsky (Micah Joseph), 137,
141, 144,-6.
Berkowitz (J. D.), 191.
Bernfeld (Simeon), 193.
Bernstein (Yehiel), 80.
Bershadsky (J.), Dumashevitsky), 184f.
Beth ha-Midrash, 150, 153f. (See Gloss. 2.)
Beth ha-Otzar, 25
Beth Yehudah, 24.
Between Sea and Sea, 189.
Between Two Mountains, 140.
Beyond Life, 186.
Beyond the Frontiers, 187, 189.
Bialik (Hayyim Nachman), 131, 148, 163, 174, 176, 180, 181.
Bible, Study of the, 1.
Bikkurē ha-Ittim, 15.
"Bilu," 106.
Bi'ur, The, 5, 21.
Blood Accusation, The, 25.
Boker Or, ha-, 64
Brainin (Reuben), 81, 137.
Brandstaedter (Mordecai David), 78.
Braudes (Reuben Asher), 64, 115ff., 120.
Brenner (Joseph Hayyim), 187-9.
Broken Soul, 186.
Burden of Nemirov, 149, 160f., 176.
Burial of an Ass, 98.
Burla (J.), 192.
Byron, 14.
Cabbalah, 11, 19, 25, 80, 191 (See Gloss. 3).
Carmel, ha-, 59.
Castiglione (Issac Hayyim), 19.
Christianity, 17, 124.
Circumcision, 177.
Close of Sabbath, The, 177.
Cohen (Jacob), 178f.
Come, My Love! 79.
Confession, The, 101.
Dal Mevin, 30.
Daniel Deronda, 99.
Daniel Shafranov. 191.

200

Dar'khe ha-Mishnah, 81.
David and Barzillai, 43f.
David and Michal, 42.
Davidovitch (J. L.), 138.
Dead of the Desert, The, 149, 154-6.
Deianira, 170.
Destruction of Troy, 33.
Div're Shalom v'Emeth, 6.
Dolitzky (Menahem), 110f.
Dor Dor v'Dor'shav, 80f.
Dr. Joseph Alfasi, 78.
Dubno (Solomon), 5.
Efes Damim, 25.
Ehrenpreis (M.), 137.
Elhanan, 79.
"George Eliot," 99.
Emeth, ha-, 63.
Epistolæ obscurorum virorum, 13.
Erlkönig, 79.
Erter (Isaac), 11ff., 25, 103.
Eternal People, The, 89ff.
Euchel (Isaac), 4.
Fall of the Tzaddik's House, 140.
Fathers and Sons, 55, 130.
Faust, 14.
Feierberg (Mordecai Zevi), 97, 102, 143f., 150.
Fichmann (Jacob), 182f.
First Principles of Learning, 5.
Flying Letters, 130.
Four Generations—Four Deaths, 140.
Four Precious Stones, 140.
Four Hundred Years Ago, 135f.
Franco-Mendes (David), 8.
Frankel (Zachariah), 81f.
Friemann-Liebermann (A.), (See " Bar-Derora.")
Frischmann (David), 109, 129f.
From the Stock of Israel, 79.
From Here and There, 189.
From East and West, 137.
From the Mouth of the People, 140.
Fuenn (Samuel Joseph), 59.
Galuth (See Gloss. 4).
Gan Na'ul, 5.
Geiger (Abraham), 9, 15.
Gemara (See Gloss. 5).
Genesin (E. N.), 190f.
Germany, Jews of, 1ff., 86f.

Getting Less, 140.
Ginzberg (Asher), (See "Ahad Ha-Am").
Goldenberg (S. L.), 15.
Gordon (David), 92.
Gordon (Judah Lob), 42-4, 61, 64-77, 85, 103, 107, 145.
Gottlober (Abraham Baer), 64.
Graeber (Eisig), 109.
Grünberg (U. Z.), 193.
Günzburg (Mordecai Aharon), 21, 26-8, 85.
Hakkafoth, 177.
Hakohen (Mordecai ben Hillel), 80.
Hakohen (Shalom), 15.
Halevy (Joseph), 137.
Happy Poor, The, 135.
Hasas (H.), 192.
Hashkaphah, 104.
Hasidim, 11, 13, 25, 55, 78, 89, 96, 141, 147, 192 (See Gloss. 6).
Haskalah, 4, 16, 21, 24, 26f., 31, 48, 56, 59, 64, 68, 83, 85, 91, 94, 100, 105, 107, 110, 135, 137 (See Gloss. 7).
Heat of the Day, The, 177.
Hebrew Language, 1ff., 56, 77, 125, 129, 131.
Hebrew Language, Modernising of the, 104, 125.
Hebrew Language, Revival of Spoken, 102f,
Hebrew Melodies, 14.
Heder, 1, 27, 94, 186, 188 (See Gloss. 8).
He-Halutz, 13, 15.
Heker Davar, 57.
Hellenism, 17f., 147f., 161.
Hero Shemaiah, The, 140.
Herzl (Theodor), 122f.
Hibbath-Zion Movement, 80, 100ff., 106f., 110, 123, 126.
Hidden Melodies, 179.
Hillel, 105.
Hope, The (Ha-Tikvah), 111f.
Horowitz (S. I.), 146f.
I believe, 178.
Ibn Ezra, 11.
If I Forget Thee, 110.
If Thou Wouldst Know, 150.

I have desired of Thee, 110.
I know a Damsel, Beautiful and Tender, 179.
Imber (Herz), 111f.
In a Summer House, 140.
In Depression, 140.
Inheritance, The, 98.
In the City of Slaughter, 149, 160f., 174.
In the Clefts of the Rock, 166.
In the Depths of the Sea, 66-8.
In the Lion's Jaws, 68-71.
In the Mountains, 181.
In those Days, 130.
In Winter, 187f.
Italy, Hebrew Literature in, 15ff.
It Ends in Smoke, 146.
It shall come to pass in the Latter Days, 180.
Jael and Sisera, 35ff.
Jawitz (Zev), 118-120, 185.
Jew-hater of Gryleff, 78.
Jochanan ben Zakkai, 145.
Jordanite, The, 182.
Joseph II, Emperor of Austria, 6.
Jost (Isaac Marcus), 9.
Journey to Palestine in the Year 2040, 183.
Judah ha-Levi, 10, 18, 19, 39, 147.
Kabak (A. A.), 191.
Kahana (David), 80.
Kantor (Judah Löb), 79, 109.
Katzenelsohn (Isaac), 183.
Kerem Hemed, 15.
King of Terrors, 79.
Kinnor Bath Tziyon, 33, 40.
Kinnor Na'im, 19.
Klatzkin (J.), 193.
K'neseth Israel, 109.
Kol, ha-, 63.
Kovner (Uri), 57.
Krochmal (Abraham), 10, 13.
Krochmal (Nachman), 9ff., 15.
Kuzari, ha-, 10, 18.
Laughing Generation, The, 179.
Law, The and Philosophy, 19.
Law from Heaven, The, 19.
Leah the Fishwife, 135.
Lebensohn (Dov Hakohen), (See "Adam Hakohen").
Lebensohn (Micah Joseph), 32-41, 79.
Let Him Remember, 130.
Letteris (Meir Halevi), 14f.
Letters on Literature, 129f.
Let There Be Criticism! 58.
Levinsohn (Isaac Dov), 21ff.
Levinsky (Elhanan Löb), 183.
Lewin (Judah Löb), 63, 78f.
Lilienblum (Moses Löb), 59ff., 103, 130.
Lindau (Baruch), 5.
Literature and Life, 136.
Little Fables for Grown-up Children, 73.
Lolli (Ehud), 19.
Long Letter, 187.
Love, 190.
Love and Duty, 135.
Luther, 91.
Luzzatto (Moses Hayyim), 4.
Luzzatto (Samuel David), 15-19, 35, 93, 97.
Ma'aseh, 181f.
Maggid, ha- 58f.
Maimonides, 16, 17, 90.
Mandelkern (Solomon), 79.
Mané (Mordecai Zevi), 112ff.
Mapu (Abraham), 45ff., 103, 131.
Maskilim, 2, 6, 42, 62, 72, 84f., 102, 105ff., 118, 126, 141, 185 (*See* Haskalah).
Matmid, ha-, 149, 151f.
Meassef, ha-, 4f., 15.
Mebo ha-Yerushalmi, 81.
Megalleh Temirin, 13.
Melitz, ha-, 59ff., 109.
Melitzah, 4, 15 (*See* Gloss. 10).
Menahem the Scribe, 135.
"Mendelé Mocher Sefarim," 130ff., 141, 177.
Mendelssohn (Moses), 4, 90.
Meshi ("Silk"), 186.
Midrash, 131.
Mish'lé Yehudah, 66.
Mishnah, 2, 131 (*See* Gloss. 11).
Mistress Hannah, 140.
Modern Guide to the Perplexed, 9.
Modern Melodies, 140.
Molière, 31.

Mordecai Kizowitch, 78.
Morpurgo (Rachel), 19.
Mourning Dove, The, 14.
Muhammad, 166.
Musings on Things of Old, 167.
My Mare, 130, 133.
My Soul's Desire, 113f.
Nationalism, Jewish, 17, 88ff.
Neginoth minni Kedem, 120.
Neumark (David), 147f.
Nietzsche (Friedrich), 123f., 144f., 170, 176.
Night of Terror, 140.
Nocturno, 168.
Nordau (Max), 123.
Oholé Shem, 26.
Old People, 186.
Old Wine in New Bottles, 58.
On the Hills of Zion, 110.
On the Threshold of the House of Study, 150.
Organ, The, 138.
Or, ha-, 104.
Otzar ha-Sifruth, 109.
Otzar Nehmad, 15.
Pancakes, The, 177.
Paperna (Abraham Jacob), 58.
Peretz (Isaac Löb), 93, 138ff.
Perl (Joseph), 13.
Perurim, 121.
Pessimist and Optimist, 30.
"Petachiah (Jacob Obadiah ben)," 13.
Pines (Yehiel Michal), 93f., 97, 118, 185.
Point of a Yod, The, 74ff.
Pool, The, 149.
Practical Ability, 79.
Praise be to the Righteous, 4, 31.
Prophets, Study of the, 1, 2, 22.
Queen of the Morning, 179.
Rabinovitz (Saul Phineas), 109.
Racine, 8, 14.
Rapoport (Solomon Judah), 8f.
Rashi, 19.
Rebbis, 11, 25 (See Hasidim).
Reform movement, 85ff, 90f.
Reggio (Isaac Samuel), 19.
Religion and Life, 64, 115.

Religion, Jewish, 90, 118f., 147.
Reward of the Righteous, 98.
Rose of Sharon, 57.
Round about the Point, 187f.
Rubin (Solomon), 80.
Rudermann (Pesach), 80.
Ruffians, 179.
Russia, Jews in, 21ff., 84f.
Sachs (Senior), 15.
Satanov (Isaac), 5.
Schorr (Josua Heschel), 13, 15, 16.
Schulman (Eleazar), 79.
Schulman (Kalman), 57.
"Science of Judaism," 9.
Scroll of Fire, 149, 162.
"Secco (M.)" (Meir Smelansky), 192
Shabbethai Zevi, 80, 155.
Shadows, The, 143.
Shahar, ha-, 61, 63, 73, 78ff., 87f., 92, 99.
Shalkowitch (Abraham Leib), (See "Ben Avigdor").
"Shalom Aleichem," 191.
Shapira (Constantine Asher), 109f.
Shapira (Herrmann), 137.
Shelomoh Molko, 191,
Shiloach, ha-, 79-80, 125, 137, 183.
Shimonovitz (David), 182.
Shiré Bath Tziyon, 33.
Shiré Tif'ereth, 6.
Shlionsky (A.), 193.
Shneur (Z.), 178ff.
Shofmann (G.), 187, 189f.
Shomereth Yabam, 77.
Shulamith, 57.
Shulhan Arukh, 60, 64, 74, 76. (See Gloss. 13.)
Sick Berelé, The, 177.
Sidonia, 78.
Sifrè Agorah, 134.
Sihoth minni Kedem, 120.
Silbermann (Eliezer), 58.
Sins of Youth, 62.
Slonimsky, (Hayyim Selig), 59.
Smelansky (Meir). (See "M. Secco.")
Smilansky (Moses), (Khaja Musa), 191.
Smolenskin (Peretz), 58, 61, 86—93, 131.

Socialists, Hebrew, 63.
Sokolow (Nahum), 109.
Solomon and Ecclesiastes, 33ff.
Song of Exiles, 173.
Song of Perdition, The, 149.
Songs of Israel, 180.
Songs of Jeshurun, 110.
Songs of Judah, 65.
Songs in the Holy Language, 31.
Songs of Splendour, 149.
Sons of Arabia, 191.
Sons of My Spirit, 93.
Soul of Hasidim, The, 140-1.
Souvenirs, 187.
Spinoza, 105.
Spiritual Zionism, 123, 146, 193.
Steinberg (Jacob), 183.
Steinberg (Judah), 131, 141.
Steinmann (A.), 192f.
Stone of Darkness, The, 80.
Stone of Israel, The, 88.
Stone of Stumbling, The, 80.
Stone of the Wanderers, The, 80.
Strains of the Mandoline, 180.
Sunset, 179.
Tales of Spring, 164.
Talmud, 1, 3, 8, 9, 14, 23, 27, 60f., 81, 104, 120, 150, 188. (See Gemara, Mishnah).
Talmud Leshon Ivri, 5.
Tannaim, 82, 145. (See Gloss. 15).
Tartar Song, 166.
Tchernichovsky (Saul), 41, 148, 163-178, 179ff.
Teaching of Elisha ben Abuya, 63.
Temptation of Spring, The, 186.
Te'udah b'Yisrael, 24.
This too is God's Chastisement, 158f.
Thought, The, and the Violin, 140.
Thoughts and Deeds, 183.
Three that Ate, The, 130.
Tibbon, Ibn, 104.
Time to Plant, 89, 91.
Tower of Strength, The, 4, 31.
Transmutation of Melody, The, 141.
Travels of Benjamin the Third, 130.
Treasury, The, 57.

Truth and Faith, 31, 55.
"Tushiyah" Publishing Company, 138.
Two Camps, 146.
Two Extremes, 115ff.
Two Josephs ben Simeon, 77.
Tzaddiks, 11, 25, 78. (See Hasidim).
Tzefirah, ha-, 59, 109.
Tzeror Perahim, 57.
Tzevi, ha-, 104.
Vale of Weeping, The, 130.
Vengeance of a Barrel-Organ, 190.
Vengeance of the Covenant, The, 98.
Verily the People is Grass, 156, 159.
Victory, 191.
Vineyard by Night, 182.
Vision of Desolation, 182.
Visions of the Daughter of my People, 109.
Visions of False Prophets, 170, 173.
Wanderer out of Time, The, 182.
Wanderer through the Paths of Life, The, 94ff.
Watchman of the House of Israel, 11f.
Ways of Old, 57.
Weiss (Isaac Hirsch), 80f.
Wessely (Naphtali Hirsch), 5ff
Whither?, 143.
Whose House is Filled with Joy, 140.
Winchefsky (W.) (See "Ben-Netz".)
Without a Goal, 184.
Wood Magic, 168.
Yeshivah, 1, 27, 94, 95, 96, 151, 188. (See Gloss. 17).
Yiddish, 1, 6, 77, 125, 130, 131, 139, 191. (See Gloss. 18).
Young and Old we will go, 107.
Zedekiah in Prison, 71f., 145.
Zederbaum (Alexander), 59.
Zeitlin (Hillel), 141.
Zerubbabel, 25.
Zionism, 19, 41f., 48, 92, 98, 119, 121ff., 129, 185, 188, 191.
Zionist Congress, First, 156.